Assessing Conditions
to Enhance Educational
Effectiveness

GEORGE D. KUH
JILLIAN KINZIE
JOHN H. SCHUH
ELIZABETH J. WHITT

Assessing Conditions to Enhance Educational Effectiveness

The Inventory for Student Engagement and Success

A companion volume to *Student Success in College: Creating Conditions That Matter*

JOSSEY-BASS
A Wiley Imprint
www.josseybass.com

Published by Jossey-Bass
A Wiley Imprint
989 Market Street, San Francisco, CA 94103-1741   www.josseybass.com

Jossey-Bass books and products are available through most bookstores. To contact Jossey-Bass directly call our Customer Care Department within the U.S. at 800-956-7739, outside the U.S. at 317-572-3986, or fax 317-572-4002.

Jossey-Bass also publishes its books in a variety of electronic formats. Some content that appears in print may not be available in electronic books.

Library of Congress Cataloging-in-Publication Data

Assessing conditions to enhance educational effectiveness : The inventory for student engagement and success / George D. Kuh ... [et al.].— 1st ed.
    p. cm.
  Includes bibliographical references.
  ISBN-13: 978-0-7879-8220-1 (alk. paper)
  ISBN-10: 0-7879-8220-2 (alk. paper)
  1. College student orientation—United States. 2. Education, Higher—United States—Evaluation. I. Kuh, George D.
  LB2343.32.A76 2005
  378.1'98—dc22

                 2005013832

Printed in the United States of America
FIRST EDITION
PB Printing   10 9 8 7 6 5 4 3 2 1

CONTENTS

PREFACE

All colleges and universities can improve the quality of their teaching and student learning. The trick is figuring out how to do it.

In *Student Success in College,* we described 20 very different colleges and universities, all of which had better-than-predicted levels of undergraduate student engagement and graduation rates (Kuh, Kinzie, Schuh, Whitt, & Associates, 2005). We concluded that no single blueprint exists for becoming a high-performing institution, one that is committed to student success and aligns its policies and practices to achieve that end. We also concluded that there is no one best way to estimate how effective an institution is; many methods are available. Yet, most colleges and universities face challenges at three key points when taking stock of their performance:

- Launching a comprehensive examination of institutional effectiveness
- Sustaining the effort over an extended period of time
- Taking action to address the results of the examination

In this volume, we offer a framework to help institutions work through these difficult points along the road to improvement. We also believe that by adapting and using our suggested protocols, a college or university can make progress toward desired institutional change.

The Inventory for Student Engagement and Success (ISES) is a template for institutions to use with *Student Success in College* (Kuh et. al., 2005) to examine what they are doing, how well they are doing it, and where they are falling short in creating the conditions for student success. The ideas come from extensive experience working in and studying postsecondary institutions, both on a national scale and in-depth analyses of individual colleges and universities.

Developing ISES was prompted by two large scale projects separated by more than a decade. In 1988–89, three of us worked with other colleagues on a study of 14 institutions we reported on in *Involving Colleges* (Kuh, Schuh, Whitt, & Associates, 1991). After that book appeared, other institutions requested that we conduct what we called "culture audits"—in-depth studies of aspects of campus life that encouraged students to take advantage of high-quality out-of-class learning opportunities. We held workshops for member institutions from the New Hampshire College and University Council, a consortium of colleges and universities in Ohio, the Virginia Involving Colleges Audit Project, and a dozen or so schools of the Coalition of Christian Colleges and Universities. We also used the audit process to conduct studies of student life and institutional cultures on many campuses in the United States and Canada. And we wrote a fair amount about some of these experiences (Kuh, 1990, 1993; Kuh & Andreas, 1991; Kuh, Schuh, & Whitt, 1991; Schuh & Kuh, 1991; Whitt, 1993, 1996; Whitt & Kuh, 1991).

Recently, we studied the 20 strong-performing schools described in *Student Success in College*. In addition to learning more about the conditions associated with student engagement and persistence, we also learned more about how to gauge whether these important properties exist at a college or university. We share these lessons in this volume by focusing on how an institution can look at itself critically and determine where effort is needed to enhance student success.

Acknowledgments

We are indebted to the marvelous research team that helped collect the data for the Documenting Effective Educational Practice (DEEP) project, which was the basis for *Student Success in College* and this book. They are: Charles Blaich, Anne Bost, Larry Braskamp, Ed Chan, Arthur Chickering, Jason De Sousa, Elaine El-Khawas, Sara Hinkle, Mary Howard-Hamilton, Bruce Jacobs, Adrianna Kezar, Richard Lynch, Peter Magolda, Kathleen Manning, Carla Morelon, Shaila Mulholland, Richard Muthiah, Charles Schroeder, and Mary Beth Snyder. We benefited, too, from the wise counsel of our partners at the American Association for Higher Education, especially Barbara Cambridge. Along the way we received splendid advice from Daryl Smith and Ted Marchese. In addition, Rob Aaron helped us with one of the later site visits and with many details in preparing the final ISES manuscript.

We could not have undertaken DEEP nor produced this volume without the generous support of Lumina Foundation for Education and the Center of Inquiry in the Liberal Arts at Wabash College.

Finally, although these good people and organizations were essential to our work, we are responsible for the contents. We sincerely hope you find our suggestions helpful and put them to good use.

July 2005

George D. Kuh
Indiana University
Bloomington, Indiana

Jillian Kinzie
Indiana University
Bloomington, Indiana

John H. Schuh
Iowa State University
Ames, Iowa

Elizabeth J. Whitt
The University of Iowa
Iowa City, Iowa

ABOUT THE AUTHORS

JILLIAN KINZIE is associate director of the NSSE Institute for Effective Educational Practice and Project Manager of the Documenting Effective Educational Practice (DEEP) initiative. She earned her Ph.D. in higher education with a minor in women's studies at Indiana University Bloomington. Prior to this, she held a visiting faculty appointment in Higher Education and Student Affairs at Indiana University where she coordinated the master's program. She worked as assistant dean at the School of Interdisciplinary Studies, Western College Program at Miami University (Ohio) and as an administrator in student affairs for several years.

In 2001, she was awarded a Student Choice Award for Outstanding Faculty at Indiana University. Kinzie has coauthored *Continuity and Change in College Choice: National Policy, Institutional Practices and Student Decision Making*, and *The Learning-Centered Classroom: What Does Learning Theory Have to Say?* She has conducted research on undergraduate women in science, retention of underrepresented students, and student engagement at women's colleges.

GEORGE D. KUH is Chancellor's Professor of Higher Education at Indiana University Bloomington where he directs the Center for Postsecondary Research. He received his B.A. from Luther College, M.S. from the St. Cloud State University, and Ph.D. from The University of Iowa. At Indiana University, he served as chairperson of the Department of Educational Leadership and Policy Studies, Associate Dean for Academic Affairs in the School of Education, and Associate Dean of the Faculties for the Bloomington campus.

George's interests include assessment, student engagement, institutional improvement, and campus cultures. He has consulted with more than 160 institutions of higher education and educational agencies in the United States and abroad. He is a past president of the Association for the Study of Higher Education (ASHE) and serves on the editorial boards of *Change* and *Liberal Education*. George has received awards for his research contributions from the American College Personnel Association (ACPA), Association for Institutional Research, ASHE, Council of Independent Colleges, and National Association of Student Personnel Administrators. He also received the Virginia B. Smith Innovative Leadership Award from the National Center on Public Policy and Higher Education and Council for Adult and Experiential Learning, the Educational Leadership Award for Teaching from St. Cloud State University, and Indiana University's prestigious Tracy Sonneborn Award for a distinguished record of scholarship and teaching.

JOHN H. SCHUH is Distinguished Professor of Educational Leadership at Iowa State University. He has held administrative and faculty assignments at Wichita State University, Indiana University Bloomington, and Arizona State University. He earned his B.A. degree in history from the University of Wisconsin-Oshkosh, and his M.C. in college counseling and student affairs administration and Ph.D. degree in higher education from Arizona State. He is the author, coauthor, or editor of more than 200 publications, including 22 books and monographs, 60 book chapters, and 102 articles. Among these are *Foundations of Student Affairs Practice* (with Florence Hamrick and Nancy Evans) and *Involving Colleges* (with George Kuh, Elizabeth Whitt, and Associates). He is editor-in-chief of the New Directions for Student Services Sourcebook Series and is associate editor of the *Journal of College Student Development*.

Schuh has made over 210 presentations and speeches to campus-based, regional, and national meetings and has served as a consultant to 50 colleges, universities, and other organizations. Among his many honors, Schuh has received the Contribution to Knowledge Award and the Presidential Service Award from the American College Personnel Association, and the Contribution to Literature or Research Award from the National Association of Student Personnel Administrators.

ELIZABETH J. WHITT is a professor in the College of Education at The University of Iowa and coordinator of Graduate Programs in Student Affairs Administration. She received her B.A. degree in history from Drake University, M.A. in college student personnel administration from Michigan State University, and Ph.D. in higher education administration and sociology from Indiana University Bloomington. Whitt served on the faculties at Oklahoma State University, Iowa State University, and University of Illinois at Chicago. She also worked in residence life and student affairs administration at Michigan State University, University of Nebraska-Lincoln, and Doane College (Nebraska).

Whitt is associate editor of the New Directions for Student Services monograph series and served on the editorial boards of the *Journal of College Student Development,* the *NASPA Journal,* and the *Review of Higher Education.* She received the Early Career Scholar Award from the Association for the Study of Higher Education in 1995 and, in 1999, the Annuit Coeptis Senior Professional Award from ACPA and the Robert H. Shaffer Distinguished Alumnus/na Award from the Department of Higher Education and Student Affairs at Indiana University. In 2002, ACPA named her a Senior Scholar for her contributions to student affairs research and practice.

Assessing Conditions to Enhance Educational Effectiveness

PART ONE

Student Success in College

Why It Matters and What Institutions Can Do About It

Are you satisfied with your institution's graduation rates?

To what extent does your institution challenge and support students and foster their learning and personal development? How do you know?

What might you do differently to improve student learning and persistence on your campus?

This monograph sets forth a framework for answering these and related questions. It can help you assess the conditions on your campus associated with student success in college. The process outlined in the Inventory for Student Engagement and Success (ISES) can be helpful in other ways as well:

- Energizing institutional improvement or strategic planning efforts

- Informing self-studies for accreditation and program reviews

- Obtaining information pertinent to student learning outcomes assessments and related aspects of institutional performance

Those at your institution responsible for these kinds of activities will benefit from knowing the extent to which conditions for student success exist on your campus. Using ISES can provide you and your colleagues with information to help inform policy and decision making.

What's to Come

The first two chapters provide the rationale for assessing the conditions that matter to student success. Chapter One reviews why so much attention is paid to student success and describes the project on which ISES is based. Chapter Two discusses principles for using the Inventory productively. The diagnostic queries in Chapter Three will help determine the extent to which your institution has its own versions of the six properties and conditions common to high-performing schools in place and how well they are working together to create a campus culture that fosters student success. Chapter Four offers a complementary set of diagnostic queries that addresses the five clusters of effective educational practices featured on the National Survey of Student Engagement. Chapters Three and Four present ISES as a comprehensive, systematic, institution-wide analysis. But ISES also can be used to examine conditions related to student success associated with segments of an institution, such as a college within in a large university, a student affairs division or a unit within the division. Chapter Five illustrates ways the information generated from the ISES process can be used, including accreditation self-studies, faculty and governing board retreats, and planning processes.

CHAPTER 1

Why Focus on Student Success?

Interest in creating the conditions that enhance student learning and supporting students in achieving their educational goals is at an all-time high. The pool of prospective undergraduates is wider, deeper, and more diverse than ever, and four-fifths of high school graduates need some form of postsecondary education to acquire the knowledge, skills, and competencies necessary to address increasingly complex social, economic, and political issues. Baccalaureate attainment rates vary widely from one institution to another. For example, about 20% of all four-year colleges and universities graduate less than one-third of their first-time, full-time, degree-seeking, first-year students within six years (Carey, 2004). The best predictors of whether a student will graduate are academic preparation and motivation (Adelman, 2004; Pascarella & Terenzini, 2005). Therefore, institutions might be tempted to focus on increasing selectivity and recruiting "the best and the brightest" students. But admitting only the best-prepared students is a tactic only a few institutions can afford to pursue. Moreover, it is not an approach that expands access or addresses the human capital needs of individuals or society.

Student Engagement: A Key to Student Success

The extensive body of research on student development suggests another way to improve the chances that a student will succeed in college: focus on student engagement. What students *do* during college generally matters more to what they learn and whether they persist to graduation than who they are or even where they go to college. According to Pascarella and Terenzini (2005, p. 602):

> One of the most unequivocal conclusions drawn from both our previous synthesis and the research during the 1990s is that the impact of college is largely determined by individual effort and involvement in the academic, interpersonal, and extracurricular offerings on a campus. Students are not passive recipients of institutional efforts to "educate" or "change" them, but rather bear a major responsibility for any gains derived from their postsecondary experience. This is not to say that an individual campus's ethos, policies, and programs are unimportant. Quite the contrary. But if, as it appears, individual effort or engagement is the critical determinant of the impact of college, then it is important to focus on the ways in which an institution can shape its academic, interpersonal, and extracurricular offerings to encourage *student engagement.* (emphasis added)

Engagement has two key components. The first is the amount of time and effort students put into their studies and other activities that lead to the experiences and outcomes that constitute student success. The second is the ways an institution allocates its human and other resources and organizes learning opportunities and services to encourage students to participate in and benefit from such activities.

High levels of student engagement are associated with a wide range of educational practices and conditions, including purposeful student-faculty contact, active and collaborative learning, and institutional environments that are perceived by students as inclusive and affirming and where expectations for performance are clearly communicated and set at reasonably high levels (Astin, 1991; Chickering & Gamson, 1987; Chickering & Reisser, 1993; Kuh, Schuh, Whitt, & Associates, 1991; Pascarella, 2001; Pascarella & Terenzini, 1991, 2005). These and other factors and conditions are related to student satisfaction, learning and development on a variety of dimensions, persistence, and educational attainment (Astin, 1984, 1985, 1993; Bruffee, 1993; Goodsell, Maher, & Tinto, 1992; Johnson, Johnson, & Smith, 1991; McKeachie, Pintrich, Lin, & Smith, 1986; Pascarella & Terenzini, 1991, 2005; Pike, 1993; Sorcinelli, 1991). Therefore, high levels of student engagement are necessary for and contribute to collegiate success.

All this leads to a central question: Are some colleges and universities unusually effective at engaging their students? Do they "add value" to their students' experiences by inducing them to put forth more effort in activities that contribute to their learning and personal development than the students would on their own? If so, what are these schools and what can we learn from them about creating powerful learning environments for all students?

The Documenting Effective Educational Practice (DEEP) project sought to answer these questions.

Project DEEP: A Window into Effective Educational Practice_____

The purposes of Project DEEP were to discover and describe the policies and practices of institutions with strong records of student success and to share the findings with other colleges and universities that aspire to enhance the quality of undergraduate experiences. First, we identified institutions that performed well in two areas: student engagement and graduation rates. Their scores on the National Survey of Student Engagement (NSSE) were higher than predicted: they generally performed better than expected, given their student and institutional characteristics. These institutions also graduated students at a rate higher than predicted, after accounting for factors such as institutional size and selectivity and student characteristics. In this sense, higher-than-predicted levels of engagement and graduation rates represent something meaningful beyond what students bring to college: students at these institutions were taking advantage of the educational opportunities they encountered. In addition, for the results of the project to be applicable to an array of colleges and universities, the institutions we studied should—to the extent possible—reflect a wide range of characteristics, such as selectivity, location, size, and type.

Project DEEP Colleges and Universities

Alverno College (WI)

California State University at Monterey Bay (CA)

The Evergreen State College (WA)

Fayetteville State University (NC)

George Mason University (VA)

Gonzaga University (WA)

Longwood University (VA)

Macalester College (MN)

Miami University (OH)

Sewanee: The University of the South (TN)

Sweet Briar College (VA)

University of Kansas (KS)

University of Maine at Farmington (ME)

University of Michigan (MI)

University of Texas at El Paso (TX)

Ursinus College (PA)

Wabash College (IN)

Wheaton College (MA)

Winston-Salem State University (NC)

Wofford College (SC)

The 20 institutions in the DEEP study are a subset of a larger number that met the criteria of higher-than-predicted student engagement scores and graduation rates. The schools are diverse in mission, selectivity, size, control, location, and student characteristics. Nine are private, 11 are public. They are located in all regions of the country. Some are research-extensive universities; others focus exclusively on undergraduate education. Alverno, George Mason, the University of Texas at El Paso (UTEP), and California State University at Monterey Bay (CSUMB) enroll substantial numbers of commuting and part-time students. Most of the small colleges and Gonzaga, Longwood, and Miami are primarily residential. Sweet Briar College has fewer than 700 undergraduate students, whereas the University of Kansas and the University of Michigan enroll more than 20,000. Fayetteville State University and Winston-Salem State University are historically black universities. CSUMB and UTEP are Hispanic-serving institutions. Alverno and Sweet Briar are women's colleges; Wabash is a men's college. CSUMB is less than 15 years old; George Mason is less than 30. Many others were founded in the 19th century. At all but a few, the range of student ability and academic preparation is substantial. Although standardized test scores place the University of Michigan and Miami University among the most selective public universities in the country, other institutions, such as Fayetteville State University and UTEP, enroll many students who have marginal preparation for college-level work. The private colleges in the study practice selective admissions to varying degrees.

From September 2002 through December 2003, the 24 Project DEEP researchers, in groups of two to five, conducted two multiple-day visits at each of the 20 campuses. The study team reviewed countless documents and Web sites prior to, during, and after the site visits. During 1,000+ hours on these campuses, researchers observed more than 50 classrooms and laboratories, sat in on faculty and staff meetings, and talked with more than 2,700 people at the institutions—many of them more than once—to learn what these schools do to promote student success. The stories of these 20 colleges and universities are described in detail in *Student Success in College: Creating Conditions That Matter* (Kuh, Kinzie, Schuh, Whitt, & Associates, 2005).

Putting DEEP to Work

How can other colleges and universities benefit from the examples of effective educational practices in these different institutional settings? The Inventory for Student Engagement and Success (ISES) is intended to guide administrators, faculty, staff, and students in evaluating institutional policies and practices with an eye on student success. Familiarity with the concepts discussed in *Student Success in College* is essential for using ISES effectively.

ISES concentrates on the elements the DEEP institutions have in common and elements that are distinctive to their missions, settings, and students. By asking questions such as "What are we doing?" and "Why are we doing it this way?" people can determine the relevance and responsiveness of their institution's policies and practices to the changing needs and interests of students and to evolving institutional and external conditions.

The ISES process has other benefits. The systematic examination of the quality of undergraduate education brings people together to talk seriously about the factors and conditions that promote student success. In addition, the results of such examination have a variety of applications. Alverno College, for example, is using the six conditions common to strong-performing schools as an organizing framework for its North Central Association self-study.

Are You Ready for ISES?

Readiness inventories help determine whether people are adequately prepared to successfully undertake a particular activity, such as children starting kindergarten or couples contemplating marriage. Assuming you have a clear understanding of the results of the DEEP study as described in *Student Success in College,* we offer six questions that focus on the state of mind of key players and the climate for institutional change to help you estimate your institution's "readiness" for ISES:

1. Who in the university community is interested in and willing to address the institutional challenges related to student success, and to what extent are they willing and able to commit time to using ISES and the findings?

2. To what extent are institutional leaders, such as the president, provost, vice president for student affairs, and vice president for financial affairs, supportive of using ISES to identify and address areas in need of improvement? Are student leaders disposed to participate?

3. Given the size and complexity of your institution, what would constitute a critical mass of interest and commitment to use ISES? Is that critical mass available?

4. What human and fiscal resources would be necessary to initiate and keep the ISES process going? Are those resources available? What role can students play in collecting and interpreting the information?

5. Is a person or a unit willing and able to shepherd the ISES process?

6. To what extent are campus groups open to examining assumptions, answering difficult ISES questions, and receiving information that may make some uncomfortable?

There are no "right" answers to these questions. Colleges and universities differ, for example, in the nature and amount of support needed from senior leadership to launch and sustain change efforts. How much leadership support is enough to undertake ISES at *your* institution? How many people are open to asking and answering difficult questions and are the number and influence of these people sufficient? Only you and your colleagues can make these important decisions.

If you are unsure about adapting an ISES approach as part of an institutional improvement strategy, consider Karl Weick's (1995, p. 168) playful phrase, "ready, fire, aim." Weick used it to challenge the conventional wisdom that encourages spending a lot of time designing an elaborate implementation plan, which often ends up paralyzing an organization. Rather, he argues that when consequences matter it is more productive to act in ways that will produce desired outcomes. This is the case with DEEP institutions. They are action oriented; ideas and impetus for change bubble up from different places.

We hope you and your colleagues are encouraged by Weick's observation and will continue the journey toward institutional reflection and discovery, at least for a few more chapters.

CHAPTER 2

Guiding Principles
for Using the Inventory
for Student Engagement
and Success

The Inventory for Student Engagement and Success (ISES) is a guide for colleges and universities that wish to examine their educational effectiveness. This chapter discusses principles consistent with this goal. The principles represent assumptions about organizational effectiveness, student success, and what Cooperrider and Srivastva (1987) call "appreciative inquiry," an approach to discovery and understanding that recognizes students' experiences are shaped profoundly by what they *do* during college as well as their *perceptions* of their interactions with other students and the institution.

Three caveats. First, as we've noted, the Inventory and the supporting material in this volume are intended to supplement *Student Success in College: Creating Conditions That Matter* (Kuh, Kinzie, Schuh, Whitt, & Associates, 2005). A thorough understanding of the content of that book is necessary to use ISES effectively. Second, ISES is not simply a checklist of institutional practices or a set of interview questions for one-time use. It is a comprehensive, responsive template for scrutinizing your institution's policies, programs, and practices alongside the ideas described in *Student Success in College* and the literatures on student development, promising educational practices, and institutional innovation and change. Third, the diagnostic queries in ISES must be adapted to your particular institution's history, culture, circumstances, and properties.

With these caveats in mind, we offer eight principles that speak to the nature and substance of the ISES approach. Keeping these principles in mind can help make the most of the time and effort invested in using ISES.

1. Context Is Everything

> *Each person touches only one part of the elephant and therefore knows only that part. . . . One must put all of these perspectives together to get a full picture of what an elephant actually looks like. But such a picture still will be limited, even distorted, if the only place one sees the elephant is in the zoo or at the circus. To understand the elephant—how it developed, how it uses its trunk, why it is so large—one must see it on the African savanna or in the Asian jungle. In short, one must see it in context and as part of an ecological system. (Patton, 2002, p. 62)*

Michael Quinn Patton uses the familiar story of touching the elephant to illustrate the need to place something as complicated as institutional effectiveness in context to fully appreciate and understand it. This emphasis on context comports with the practices of DEEP colleges and universities that go to great lengths to create and maintain educational conditions congenial to *their* setting, including institutional mission, campus cultures, and student characteristics.

The context for ISES includes all aspects of the setting and the phenomena under study. In addition to various policies and practices, context includes physical and psychological environments, such as how space is used and how students feel they are treated; the institution's history and current state of development including its founding values, ways of responding to periods of struggle, and changes in mission or student characteristics; present circumstances, such as time of the academic year the process will unfold; the geographical location of the institution; and the characteristics of community members, including students. In this sense, "context becomes the framework, the reference point, the map . . . [It] is used to place people and action in time and space and as a resource for understanding what they say and do" (Lawrence-Lightfoot, 1997, p. 41).

2. The Whole Is Greater Than the Sum of the Parts

> *Failure to incorporate and capitalize on students' out-of-class experiences risks increasing learning only at the margins. . . . In some areas of intellectual development (including critical thinking), it is the breadth of student involvement in the intellectual and social experiences of college, rather than any particular type of involvement, that matters most. The greatest impact appears to stem from students' total level of campus engagement, particularly when academic, interpersonal, and extracurricular involvements are mutually reinforcing, and relevant to a particular educational outcome. (Pascarella & Terenzini, 2005, p. 647)*

The questions in the Inventory are not meant to suggest that educationally effective conditions and practices are discrete and independent, but that they are complementary and interdependent. Activities and behaviors in one set of conditions or one cluster of educational practices—*although important in and of themselves*—have a greater influence on learning and student success when combined with other promising approaches. Therefore, a broad, integrative perspective is needed to understand the complex system of policies, practices, and conditions that influence student success at an institution or within a program (Kuh, Schuh, Whitt, & Associates, 1991; Patton, 2002; Schuh & Upcraft, 2000) *and* the complicated, holistic nature of student learning and personal development (Banta, Lund, Black, & Oblander, 1996; Seymour, 1995; Terenzini & Pascarella, 1994). Those who seek to understand what matters to student success must focus on both the parts *and* the whole.

Also, the policies, programs, practices, and individual student, faculty, and staff behaviors identified in ISES overlap and influence one another. For example, understanding the extent to which an institution creates supportive environments for students requires focusing on support services *as well as* critically weighing institutional values, assumptions, and attitudes about academic achievement and support. Questions about the extent to which campus support services are used, by whom, and with what effects must be accompanied by questions about what messages are communicated to students about those who need and use support services.

3. Evidence Is Essential: The More, the Better

Most college campuses are awash in data but thirsty for information. (Seymour, 1995, p. 80)

DEEP schools use information about students and their learning and about other elements of institutional effectiveness for institutional accountability and improvement (Kuh et al., 2005). Indeed, these institutions seemed to be in a perpetual learning mode—monitoring where they were, what they were doing, where they wanted to go, and how to maintain momentum toward positive change.

The process outlined in ISES requires evidence generated by systematic data collection and analysis. For many faculty and staff members, the word *data* conjures daunting pictures of tables of numbers and complex statistical analyses. In fact, many questions relevant to student success can be answered—at least in part—with numbers, such as "How many first-time, full-time students persist to graduation in six years?" or "How does academic performance differ for students who do or do not use tutoring or other academic support services?" Reliable quantitative instruments, including the National Survey of Student Engagement (NSSE) and the College Student Experiences Questionnaire (CSEQ), are available to examine these important dimensions of student learning and engagement.

But useful, insightful data also can come in other forms and from other sources, including personal experiences and narratives. Qualitative research methods are particularly useful for describing and interpreting complex concepts and experiences, such as students' understanding of institutional expectations or the meaning faculty make of institutional messages about the appropriate balance of teaching and research (Magolda, 1999; Patton, 2002; Rossman & Rallis, 2003; Whitt, 1996). Pertinent sources of qualitative data include:

Documents, including campus newspapers, planning documents, students' written work, admissions materials, both print and electronic

Observations of student use of and interactions in a residence hall dining area, traffic patterns in the union, and student-faculty interactions in service learning activities

Individual interviews and focus groups of faculty, students, student affairs staff, and institutional leaders

A detailed summary of research methods used in Project DEEP, available in Appendix A of *Student Success in College,* illustrates strategies for studying aspects of students' experiences and institutional or student cultures. Sample protocols modeled after those used in Project DEEP can be found in Appendix A of this volume. Other informative sources about using qualitative methods are listed in the references.

Obtaining as much information as possible about your students and institutional policies and practices will enable you to use the Inventory productively. Equally important, ISES results will be richer and more accurate if quantitative and qualitative sources of information are combined to answer the diagnostic queries in Chapters Three and Four that guide the ISES approach. The task requires people who are, in Fullan's (2001, p. 117) words, "assessment literate." That is, they analyze student performance data critically, disaggregate the information appropriately to identify groups that may be under- or overperforming, *and* put the information to use and develop action plans.

To check the internal validity of the answers to ISES questions, ask: "How do we know? How do we know our answers are accurate? Where is the corroborating evidence?" For example, one question asks, "Are pathways to and expectations for student success clear to new students?" An instructive response to that question would include detailed reports from students about their experiences and impressions.

4. Test Prevailing Assumptions

What you expect to see is what you see. . . . Our interpretations hinge on our expectations, beliefs, and values. . . . We manage to see what we expect and want. . . . A better alternative is to think, to probe more deeply into what is really going on. (Bolman & Deal, 2003, pp. 32–33)

Because assumptions play a large role in shaping expectations, they must be identified and accounted for when trying to understand something as complex as an institution's culture and its influence on student success. One way to test assumptions is to focus questions on both small details about students' experiences and larger, institution-wide conditions. How, for example, do you assume students spend their time? What do you believe they expect of themselves and of the institution? What do they learn while in school, how do they learn best, and from whom? How might those assumptions influence "what you see" when you answer questions in ISES? How might those assumptions affect your capacity to learn "what is really going on"? What, in fact, do you "think" you know about your students that has not been corroborated recently with good data?

Questioning assumptions can make some people uncomfortable. Those managing the ISES process need to prepare for helping people with the task. Rosovsky (1990, p. 259) advises: "Never underestimate the difficulty of changing false beliefs by facts." But facts—in the form of data about students and their experiences—are essential for altering false beliefs and improving educational practice.

5. Cast a Wide Net

Assessment is no less a collective endeavor than a choir performance. Both require interaction, participation, direction, and the joining together of different voices in common song. (Banta et al., 1996, pp. 35–36)

To understand an institution, program, or practice, one must see it, hear about it, and make meaning of it from the perspectives of those who know it well (Ely & Associates, 1991; Kuh, Schuh, Whitt, & Associates, 1991; Kuh & Whitt, 1988; Martin, 2002; Merriam & Associates, 2002; Patton, 2002; Rossman & Rallis, 2003). Students' experiences, for example, cannot be fully understood and appreciated without students' interpretations. One might peruse a college's admissions view book to identify messages sent to prospective students about how the college defines success. Or one could attend new student orientation to hear what institutional agents tell incoming students about how to be successful. But to know what messages students actually *hear* about what to do to succeed in college, what the institution expects of them, and how they act on what they hear, you have to talk to students.

ISES questions should be posed to a large cross-section of people who hold different views and experiences. Avoid the temptation to seek data only from those whose views are consistent with your own or from those who are most eager to tell their stories. Avoid, too, focusing on people in leadership roles to the exclusion of those who work directly with students. Above all, seek stories from a wide array of students, including part-time students who commute and full-time students who live on campus, students not engaged in formal extracurricular activities as well as student leaders, and new students as well as returning students.

6. Use Outsiders to Ask Hard Questions

> *Often, an organization's participants will confide to an outsider what an insider is either unwilling or unable to hear. . . . Once individuals understand how people perceive one another and their organization, they will be better prepared to move particular aspects of the organization to create change. (Tierney, 1999, p. 138)*

Although insider perspectives are necessary to understand an institution, outsiders can play an important role because they can ask difficult questions more easily than insiders and bring fresh insights when making sense of the answers. Outsiders help insiders "transcend their own immersion" in the institution (Chaffee & Tierney, 1988, p. 4) and call attention to those elements that to insiders seem so common, obvious, or familiar that they might be overlooked despite their significance. Outsiders can ask naïve questions about widely held assumptions and about differences between espoused and enacted values. Faculty might, for example, view their college as having a strong academic focus and challenging students with rigorous coursework. But outsiders might hear from students that they routinely begin the weekend on Wednesday night. Insiders might take for granted that the institution is welcoming to all students, regardless of race, ethnicity, sexual orientation, or academic preparation, while outsiders notice that only White students are evident in public social spaces on campus.

7. Focus on What Matters to Student Success

> *Organizations that improve do so because they create and nurture agreement on what is worth achieving, and they set in motion the internal processes by which people progressively learn how to do what they need to do in order to achieve what is worthwhile. (Elmore in Fullan, 2001, p. 125)*

DEEP institutions are "positively restless" in that they have a strong improvement-oriented ethos (Kuh et al., 2005). When facing difficulties, such as declining resources or enrollment challenges, these schools look for ways to turn such circumstances into opportunities to enhance the quality of undergraduate experiences, instead of being paralyzed by their problems or lamenting their bad fortune. They assess whether their performance approximates their potential; they are prone to experiment and to take risks to enhance their performance and that of their students. At the same time, they avoid inappropriate comparisons with other institutions, focusing instead on implementing their educational missions to the best of their abilities, given their students and resources.

The ISES process will be most productive if those involved concentrate on enhancing the institution's capacity to improve by building on existing resources and opportunities and emphasizing collective strengths. Focusing too much on "what's wrong" can be demoralizing and dampen enthusiasm for institutional reflection and renewal. Focusing on what matters to student success, and on what is going well in the name of institutional improvement, can energize institutional agents and units to address what is not going well with renewed hope, vigor, and confidence.

8. Stay the Course

The good-to-great transformations never happened in one fell swoop. There was no single defining action, no grand program, no one killer innovation, no solitary lucky break, no miracle moment. Sustainable transformations follow a predictable pattern of buildup and breakthrough. (Collins, 2001, p. 186)

Meaningful change rarely occurs in dramatic fashion. Complex, large-scale initiatives almost never realize their grand promises. Karl Weick (1984) observed that a series of small wins will be more likely to have desired effects than a single, complex initiative might. A small win is "a concrete, complete, implemented outcome of moderate importance. By itself, one small win may seem unimportant. A series of wins at small but significant tasks, however, reveals a pattern that may attract allies, deter opponents, and lower resistance to subsequent proposals" (Weick, 1984, p. 43). An example of this is the Student Work Initiative at the University of Maine at Farmington described in Chapter Six of *Student Success in College*. Hiring just one student made for a powerful learning experience for the student worker and provided excellent service for the employing department. Hiring dozens of students created an atmosphere where students became key partners in solving chronic problems, in addition to providing extra financial resources for students and providing necessary services for the campus.

Another example is Sewanee: The University of the South, where for several years a small group of faculty had discussed more engaging ways to teach first-year courses. According to an administrator, "We knew we were ready to change our first-year curriculum after reviewing our poor results on the NSSE active and collaborative learning items. The results corroborated data from students and what several faculty members had been saying about the courses." A highly successful but limited-scale 12-credit-hour Interdisciplinary Humanities course indicated that first-year students benefited from active learning pedagogy. With some financial support and encouragement from the academic dean, a group of faculty and student affairs staff members set out to examine what might work more effectively for first-year students. This focused examination of first-year seminars expanded to a study of advising and changes in cocurricular programs described in Chapters Seven, Twelve, and Thirteen of *Student Success in College.*

Adapting these principles to your context and circumstances can help keep you on a productive line of inquiry and might even provide inspiration and motivation when you hit the unavoidable bumps on the road to institutional discovery and improvement.

PART TWO

Inventory for Student Engagement and Success

If you've read to this point, chances are you are disposed to finding out more about what the ISES process can do for your institution. The following three guidelines will help you use ISES productively.

First, be sure you are familiar with the conditions and properties found at DEEP schools described in Chapters Two through Seven in *Student Success in College*. These features are the foundation for relatively strong levels of student engagement and persistence. The six conditions are:

I. A "Living" Mission and "Lived" Educational Philosophy

II. An Unshakeable Focus on Student Learning

III. Environments Adapted for Educational Enrichment

IV. Clear Pathways to Student Success

V. An Improvement-Oriented Ethos

VI. Shared Responsibility for Educational Quality and Student Success

These institutional conditions, along with a host of complementary effective educational practices, work together at DEEP institutions to create a campus culture that fosters student success. They complement elements of their settings, including institutional histories, missions, and values and the characteristics of students and other community members. It's important that you *reinterpret and adapt* these conditions and practices *to your setting.*

Second, use the *best evidence available* to respond to the diagnostic queries on ISES. This could be in the form of institutional research, outcomes assessments, surveys of student and faculty behavior, and unit or campus self-studies.

Finally, *keep the goal in sight*. ISES requires that you cover a lot of territory. You and your colleagues will be looking at both the "trees" and "forest" of student success. The former refers to specific educational policies and programs as well as features of the learning environment that enhance or detract from student engagement, learning, persistence, and satisfaction. The latter refers to how these various properties work together to create a campus culture that encourages students to take advantage of the institution's resources for learning. In light of that, we recommend someone assume responsibility for monitoring three other important matters as the ISES process unfolds:

- What are we *not* doing that we should?
- What could we stop doing without negative consequences?
- What must we continue?
- How do you know?

Referring to these guidelines occasionally can help ensure that your institution is keeping its eye on the prize—discovering what it can do to enhance student success.

CHAPTER 3

Using ISES to Assess the Properties and Conditions Common to Educationally Effective Colleges

In this chapter, diagnostic queries will lead you through a systematic examination of institutional features and cultural properties common to the 20 DEEP colleges and universities. Open discussion of the meaning of each of the queries in your context will be instructive and useful in determining next steps for improving student success at your school.

I. A "Living" Mission and "Lived" Educational Philosophy

"Mission" refers to the overarching purposes of the institution—what it is and stands for as well as what it aspires to be. The mission establishes the tone of a college, conveys its educational purposes, and—when clear and coherent—influences all aspects of institutional life, including the policies and practices that foster student success. Every college has two missions: an *espoused mission* such as its written mission statement and an *enacted mission* or what the institution actually does and whom it serves. The enacted mission guides the daily actions of those in regular contact with students—in classrooms, student centers, libraries, and playing fields—as well as those who set institutional policy, make strategic plans and decisions, and allocate resources. Despite their differences, the missions of DEEP schools have one characteristic in common: the mission is "alive" in the sense that faculty members, administrators, staff, students, and others use it to explain their behavior and talk about what the institution is and where it is headed.

Over time, intentionally or not, a college develops a philosophy that guides thought and action in pursuit of its educational mission. The philosophy is composed of tacit understandings about what is important to the institution and its constituents, and unspoken, but deeply held, values and beliefs about students and their education. Institutional values really do shape policies and practices at DEEP schools. Key institutional leaders remind people what is important. And, although the missions and operating philosophies of DEEP schools differ considerably from one another, all offer programs and services that complement their respective missions and students' needs and abilities. Common to all is an unwavering focus on students and their learning.

Chapters One, Two, Six, and Fourteen of *Student Success in College* present detailed information about the institutional missions and philosophies operating at DEEP schools. This chapter contains vignettes from some of these institutions to illustrate some of the key policies and practices addressed by the diagnostic queries in each section.

Diagnostic Queries

Espoused and Enacted Missions

1. What is the *espoused* institutional mission? That is, what does the college or university assert its educational purposes to be?

2. To what extent do policies, programs, and practices throughout the institution reflect the espoused mission?

3. How do faculty, staff, students, administrators, and other community members describe the mission? To what extent are their descriptions similar and in what ways do they differ? To what extent do differences influence student success?

4. Is the mission clearly communicated and understood? What do institutional leaders, such as the president, provost, senior student affairs officer, senior faculty, and academic deans, say and do about the mission and values of the institution?

5. What is the institution's *enacted* institutional mission? That is, to what do people devote their time and energies? What is valued and rewarded? What do people say the institution is trying to do?

6. To what extent are the espoused and enacted missions consistent? In what ways are they inconsistent? How do the inconsistencies influence student engagement and educational effectiveness?

7. In what ways does the mission influence students' experiences? In what ways do students' experiences differ from what the mission espouses?

8. How are differences of opinion addressed about the mission or how it should be achieved? To what extent are disagreements about institutional direction addressed openly, and do they foster productive dialogue? Are pockets of dissent nurtured for their capacity to help the institution become more effective?

Values and Educational Philosophy

1. What are the institution's espoused core values about students and their education? To what extent are the espoused values *enacted*?

2. To what extent do faculty, staff, students, administrators, and other community members share these core values?

3. When, where, how, by whom, and to whom are institutional values communicated?

4. What is the institution's enacted educational philosophy? That is, what are the guiding beliefs about how learning occurs best and related assumptions about teaching and learning? Is the educational philosophy clearly communicated and understood? When, where, how, and by whom?

5. To what extent and in what ways are institutional core values operating consistently or inconsistently with the mission?

6. How do the enacted values and operating philosophy affect student learning and success?

Vignettes: Mission and Philosophy

Changing Mission, Changing Culture: The University of Texas at El Paso

The University of Texas at El Paso (UTEP) seeks to "extend the greatest possible educational access to a region that has been geographically isolated with limited economic and educational opportunities for many of its people" (http://www. utep.edu/aboututep/visionmissionandgoals.aspx). Central to its mission is a clear and unwavering focus on educational access for the people in El Paso and the surrounding region. This has not always been the case.

In the early 1970s, UTEP was bent on attracting students from affluent families in West Texas. In the mid-1980s, changing demographics of the region and the growing proportion of Hispanic students at the university led institutional leaders to envision a UTEP that would play a national role in Hispanic education and expand educational access in El Paso. Although the label of "Hispanic serving" institution was initially unsettling to many UTEP faculty, staff members, community business leaders, and others, over time university stakeholders came to embrace a mission that proclaimed pride in being a Hispanic-majority university.

In keeping with this new mission, institutional policies and practices were redesigned to nurture, challenge, and support students, many of whom are first-generation college students and for whom English is a second language. The university's culture also had to be reshaped to reflect UTEP's change in focus and educational philosophy (Kuh, 2004). Thus, UTEP serves as a model for how an institution can transform itself and its mission.

- *Is your institutional mission consistent with the characteristics of your students?*

- *What steps have been taken to strengthen the mission in the past five to ten years?*

- *Should the mission be changed? If not, why not? If the mission should change, what else must change, and how might those changes occur?*

- *What elements of culture must be adjusted to reflect this change? What elements should be preserved?*

A Deeply Rooted Commitment to Excellence: The University of Michigan

Founded in 1817, the University of Michigan (UM) has evolved into a national model of a complex, diverse, and comprehensive public institution of higher learning that supports excellence in research; provides outstanding undergraduate, graduate, and professional education; and demonstrates commitment to service through partnerships and collaboration that extend to the community, region, state, nation, and around the world. In contrast to the mission of UTEP, Michigan's mission has been stable over time. Over a 15-year period, UM invested more than $12,000,000 in comprehensive initiatives to affirm and enhance the quality of undergraduate education, including undergraduate research, residential learning communities, faculty fellow programs in residence halls, first-year colloquia, and expanded student access to a range of instructional technologies.

- *If your institution's mission has been stable over time, is there evidence to support the mission's contemporary relevance?*
- *Do most campus stakeholders generally support the mission?*
- *Do the institution's policies and practices complement the mission, and how do you know?*
- *What current activities at the institution might need to be deemphasized or eliminated to be consistent with the mission?*

II. Unshakeable Focus on Student Learning

Most colleges and universities claim to be committed to student learning. But just as not all espoused missions are enacted, student learning does not always receive the attention necessary to lead to student success. At DEEP institutions, student learning is the *raison d'être* for institutional policies, programs, practices, and the rationale for daily activities as well as broad institutional directions. DEEP institutions select community members for their commitment to student success and effective educational practices. Everyone connected with the enterprise—faculty, administrators, staff, and students—is encouraged to be both learner and teacher.

Undergirding an institutionwide commitment to student learning at DEEP schools is a "cool passion" for making the necessary changes in institutional policies and pedagogical practices to help students realize their potential. These activities include classroom-based problem solving, peer tutoring, service learning and other community-based projects, internships, and involvement in a variety of educationally purposeful activities outside of class. What all these activities have in common are opportunities for students to practice what they are learning in the classroom, develop leadership skills, and work with people from different backgrounds.

Make no mistake: sustaining an unwavering focus on student learning is labor-intensive. To foster student success, faculty, staff members, and others must "make time for students," something for which there is no substitute.

Chapters One, Three, Nine, and Fourteen of *Student Success in College* contain detailed information about how DEEP institutions maintain an unwavering focus on students and their learning.

Diagnostic Queries

Teaching for Learning

1. To what extent do instructional practices promote student engagement and student learning, in contrast to being vehicles to deliver instruction?

2. To what extent are active and collaborative learning strategies used appropriately in various size classes? Is the use of engaging pedagogies supported and rewarded?

3. How are faculty encouraged and supported to facilitate student learning?

4. To what extent are institutional resources dedicated to enhancing teaching and learning?

5. Do students receive timely, frequent feedback from faculty and staff about the quality of their performance?

6. What resources, such as teaching and learning centers, are available and used by faculty and students?

7. To what extent is commitment to student learning a criterion for recruitment, selection, preparation, and promotion of administrators, faculty, and staff?

8. To what extent and in what ways are students expected and prepared to teach and learn from one another in and out of class?

Focus on Holistic Student Development

1. To what extent and in what ways do institutional policies, practices, and programs support the academic and social development of students, inside and outside the classroom?

2. What roles do faculty, student affairs professionals, and others play in promoting student learning?

Making Time for Students

1. To what extent and in what ways are faculty and staff expected to make time for students and rewarded for doing so?

2. To what extent and in what ways does the institution encourage interaction between faculty and students outside of class?

3. What percentage of students engages frequently in educationally purposeful out-of-class interactions with faculty? Which students have these experiences and which do not?

Diverse Students and Learning Styles

1. How much do faculty and staff know about your students—all of them? What do faculty and staff members know about students' learning and engagement? What do faculty and staff *not* know about students but should?

2. To what extent are learning experiences—inside and outside classrooms—tailored to the needs, experiences, and learning styles of different groups of students? What examples can you identify?

Vignettes: Focus on Student Learning

Preparing Faculty to Teach Large Classes: University of Kansas

The University of Kansas (KU) has some large 400–500 student classes; one classroom even seats more than 1,000 students. One reason for offering these large classes is so that the university can continue to offer a reasonable number of smaller classes to contend with increasing enrollments. At the same time, these large classes present challenges to active and collaborative activities that considerable evidence indicates are associated with desired learning outcomes. Instructors of large classes at KU are chosen carefully for their commitment to working with groups of this size and are prepared to use engaging pedagogies. Resources to facilitate engagement in large classes such as electronic technologies are plentiful. In addition, teaching is underscored in new faculty recruitment and promotion and tenure decisions. The message that good teaching is a university priority is reinforced during new faculty orientation and throughout the early months of the academic year. The Center for Teaching Excellence (CTE) sponsors a wide variety of programs and services including: an annual fall "teaching summit" that attracts more than a third of the faculty; a two-day Best Practices Institute; seminars where faculty members discuss readings related to the scholarship of teaching and learning; and Faculty Fellows and Teaching Grant programs that support research aimed at improving teaching.

- *Whether or not "super size" classes are appropriate for your institution, what can be done to help faculty develop effective teaching approaches for different sizes and types of classes?*
- *Is support available to help faculty members experiment with pedagogical approaches that promise to foster greater levels of student learning and engagement, regardless of the sizes of undergraduate classes?*

Students Teaching Students: Wofford College

Peer tutors can be an inexpensive but effective way to enhance student learning. More important, the availability of tutors communicates to students who encounter difficulties that the institution is prepared to help them succeed. Peer tutoring at Wofford College takes a variety of forms, including one-to-one instruction in the Writing Lab by experienced tutors; formal presentations by tutors in seminars and community events; and informal assistance to peers outside of class. Preceptors help plan, implement, and teach in the freshman humanities-science learning communities; they receive academic credit and a modest stipend for their contributions. Tutors learn from their professors before working with peers. To recognize the educational value of being a peer educator, Wofford offers a three-credit "Independent Study in Teaching Learning Communities" course for preceptors.

- *How does your institution use peer educators?*
- *What preparation, supervision, and recognition do peer educators receive?*
- *How effective is peer tutoring for your students, and could it be improved and/or broadened in scope?*
- *If your institution does not use peer educators, why not?*
- *If such a program would be appropriate for your institution and your students, what would it take to begin one? What obstacles would need to be overcome?*

III. Environments Adapted for Educational Enrichment

"Environments" for student learning include all the physical and psychological spaces in which students live, work, and play. These settings can be more or less supportive of learning, reinforcing or contradicting the educational mission and values of the institution.

DEEP schools have designed and built learning settings on and off the campus to achieve their educational purposes. They modify physical environments on campus to create spaces and settings where teaching and learning can flourish. DEEP schools also attend to the educational implications of their psychological environments. Physical structures are adapted to reduce the psychological size of the large campuses and to encourage participation in the life of the institution at both small colleges and large universities. Moreover, they are "place-conscious," in that they recognize and exploit potential learning opportunities in their settings, including the surrounding community. DEEP institutions are full partners with their communities, linking people and resources to address issues that affect the quality of life on and off the campus. Equally important, these colleges and universities feature and support all forms of diversity—intellectual, social, political, ethnic, and racial. Extra efforts are made to welcome and affirm newcomers, including newcomers from groups historically underserved in higher education. In their classes, students encounter perspectives that reflect the range of the human experience. Students are encouraged and assisted to develop effective methods of interaction and more complex ways of thinking.

Chapters One, Four, Twelve, Thirteen, and Fourteen of *Student Success in College* present detailed information about what DEEP colleges and universities do to create learner-centered environments and use their setting to educational advantage.

Diagnostic Queries

Physical Environments

1. How do community members—students, faculty, staff, others—describe the institution's physical setting and appearance? To what extent and in what ways do they describe a "sense of place"?

2. To what extent are the physical setting and structures of the campus adapted for teaching and learning? What special features and resources for learning are present? In what ways are these resources used to support learning?

3. How do residence halls, recreational facilities, and student centers facilitate interaction between students and faculty and among students?

4. Do campus facilities encourage informal and spontaneous interaction among students? Do campus facilities encourage informal and spontaneous interaction between students and faculty?

5. Are facilities accessible to students and at convenient times? Are gathering places readily accessible in buildings and outdoors? Who uses them, when, and for what purposes? Who does not?

6. To what extent are institutional plans for renovations or new facilities consistent with institutional priorities and goals for student success?

Social-Psychological Campus Climates

1. How do students describe the campus climate or climates? In what ways do these climates influence student learning and success? How do different students describe campus climates? For example, how do students from groups historically underserved by higher education describe the campus climate?

2. To what extent do students describe a sense of belonging? To what extent do they describe a sense of alienation? What is it about the campus that contributes to or detracts from a sense of belonging?

3. In what ways are the worth and dignity of individuals and groups acknowledged and emphasized? To what extent are academic and social expectations for students and groups of students free of stereotypes? To what extent are members of historically underserved groups valued and affirmed?

4. Does the institution exhibit egalitarian or meritocratic attitudes and values about being in community? Or a combination? Are these attitudes consistent with the institutional mission and philosophy? Are these attitudes consistent with students' characteristics? How do these attitudes and values influence student learning and success?

Access to Learning Resources

1. Do all students have equal access to learning and other institutional resources? If some perceive they do not, why is this so?

2. Do certain groups of students use the institution's resources differently? In what ways do these differences influence learning?

3. What institutional policies and practices affirm and support or alienate and discourage full participation by members of historically underserved groups?

4. In what ways and to what extent does the institution use the educational resources of the surrounding community?

Vignettes: Environments for Learning

"The Place to Be": George Mason University's Johnson Center

Opened in 1996, the George W. Johnson Center at George Mason University was designed to integrate students' curricular and out-of-class learning experiences. Located in the center of the campus and designed to integrate academics with student life, the Johnson Center is a focal point for universitywide learning and an all-purpose campus hub. Students, faculty, and staff flow into and out of the building throughout the day and into the evening. Its eclectic collection of services and offices encourages formal and informal interaction between and among faculty and students. The Center's interior has the look of an international bazaar: bright flags hang from pillars, and students in national dress—North American to North African—eat, study, or just "hang out" together. The feeling is energetic and cosmopolitan, yet communal and even studious. In one student's words, the Johnson Center "is the hub of student life—the place to be." It has fulfilled its intended purposes in large part because its design included ideas and suggestions from many different campus constituent groups.

- *If your institution planned to construct or renovate a facility of this type, who would be involved?*

- *To what extent would or could such a building address the needs of a wide number of institutional constituents?*

- *How would your institution ensure that the facility stayed true to its purposes to encourage student engagement and learning?*

Human Scale by Design: Miami University

Human scale is a distinctive feature of Miami University. Although the institution is spread over more than 1,900 acres and enrolls more than 16,000 students, it feels much smaller. One reason Miami feels small is that it was designed as such. One can traverse the campus on foot in any direction in 15 minutes. Few buildings exceed three stories, and all are set back from the street, creating a sense that they are apart from the hustle of campus traffic. Residence halls are in quadrangles separated by expanses of green space. The Georgian architectural style was used for all university buildings, except the School of Interdisciplinary Studies, formerly Western College. Referring to Miami's human-scale physical plant, a staff member observed, "We have a mindset here that we're not as big as we are." The psychological size of Miami "creates an intimacy of connections you would expect at a much smaller school."

- *If your institution contemplated adding new facilities or undertaking a massive renovation, what environmental designs would complement your institution's mission and philosophy?*

- *What process would you use to create spaces to foster student engagement? What features might you use to convey human scale across several structures?*

- *How would you use green space, pedestrian walkways, and other features to create the desired atmosphere?*

- *How would campus stakeholders, including students, be involved in the design process?*

IV. Clear Pathways to Student Success

Student success is no accident. Students who thrive in college typically engage in a variety of educationally purposeful activities and use the educational resources of the campus to achieve desirable learning outcomes. To increase the odds that more students will invest time and energy in the right activities, DEEP schools do two things very well.

First, they teach students what the institution values, what successful students do, and how to take advantage of institutional resources for learning. These lessons are conveyed through programs tailored for first-year students and by organizing the first-year experience in educationally purposeful ways to support satisfactory transition and adjustment. Formal orientation activities ensure that new students do not get lost in the shuffle or struggle aimlessly. In addition, many informal events and processes communicate to new students, faculty, and staff what is valued and how things are done. These processes comprise acculturation.

Second, DEEP schools make sure their resources are compatible with the institution's educational mission, as well as student characteristics, and are available to all their students. They do this by providing redundant early warning systems, safety nets, and ongoing assessment and feedback. DEEP institutions also provide what students need *when* they need it through accessible and responsive systems that support teaching, learning, and student success. Matching resources, policies, and practices with the institution's educational purposes and student characteristics constitutes alignment.

Chapters One, Five, Eight, Thirteen, and Fourteen of *Student Success in College* contain detailed information about the different pathways to success created by DEEP colleges and universities.

Diagnostic Queries

Acculturation

Teaching Students How to Succeed

1. What messages does the institution communicate to prospective community members (students, faculty, staff) about:

   Expectations for student performance and outcomes?

   Expectations that students assume a fair share of responsibility for their learning?

2. Who communicates these messages and when? Are the messages consistent with the institution's espoused mission, values, and expectations?

3. Do all prospective community members receive the same messages?

4. What do current students, faculty, and staff recall about being newcomers? Did they feel welcome? Did they have a clear understanding of "how we do things here?" Were their understandings consistent with what the institution espouses?

5. What symbols and actions communicate to newcomers the importance of students and their learning and success?

6. Does the institution communicate high expectations for students—asking them to aspire and stretch beyond their perceived limits?

7. Are high expectations communicated to some students and not to others?

Creating a Sense of Community

1. Do all students feel a sense of "specialness" about the institution and about being its students? Or are feelings of "specialness" limited to certain groups of students?

2. What traditions and events introduce students to the values of the institution? To what extent are those traditions consistent or inconsistent with the espoused institutional values? What acculturation experiences should be added?

Alignment

Creating Pathways to Student Success

1. To what extent are resources, structures, programs, policies, and practices for student learning and development consistent with the institution's mission and students' characteristics?

2. Are various pathways to student success—what different types of students need to do to succeed—consistent with the characteristics of your students?

3. Are forms of challenge and support consistent with the needs of students and with the institution's educational priorities? Do students who need extra support receive it?

Front-loading Resources

1. To what extent are resources "front-loaded" to foster students' academic and social success? Are these experiences integrated with or tangential to the curriculum? How might they be integrated more effectively?

2. Do students learn about resources for their learning when they need them, if not before?

3. What programs assist the transition and success of students in need of additional preparation for college? To what extent are these programs used? What evidence exists to show that they are effective?

Early Warning Systems and Safety Nets

1. What policies and practices identify students at risk? To what extent are they used, in what ways, and by whom? How and for whom are they effective?

2. To what extent and in what ways are safety nets in the form of resources, programs, policies, practices, and structures for students in difficulty available and used? By whom are they used? Who does not use them?

3. To what extent are these resources, programs, policies, practices, and structures effective, and for whom?

Integration of Complementary Student Success Initiatives

1. To what extent are the institution's resources, programs, policies, practices, and structures for student success redundant and responsive? To what extent are they fragmented, unresponsive, and ineffective?

2. To what extent are the institution's formal out-of-class policies, programs, practices, resources, and facilities consistent with its educational priorities? Do they facilitate or inhibit student learning?

3. To what extent are students' out-of-class lives consistent with the institution's expectations? In what ways do students' out-of-class lives facilitate or inhibit their learning and success? Do some groups of students make particularly good or bad choices about how they spend their out-of-class time? What mechanisms—if any—identify students who are less engaged in educationally purposeful activities than they should be to succeed?

4. To what extent and in what ways are students, faculty, and staff accountable for meeting the institution's expectations? Are reward systems consistent with the institution's espoused educational priorities?

5. What groups or offices collect and disseminate information about students and their experiences? How is the information obtained, communicated, and used?

6. Where in the institution are the various "pictures" of students and their experiences brought together to create a holistic understanding of the quality of undergraduate programs?

Vignettes: Clearly Marked Pathways to Success

Experience Live: Gonzaga University

The Gonzaga Experience Live, or GEL, program is a powerful recruitment tool for Gonzaga because about 70% of the students who participate in GEL enroll at the university. GEL weekend, a spring event for prospective students, includes tours of the campus and Spokane, academic sessions, meals, a club and organization fair, evening social activities, and an overnight stay in a residence hall hosted by current students. Discussions during GEL focus on questions about how to live a moral life, a question of critical importance to student life at this Jesuit university.

Thus, GEL is the beginning of a powerful socialization process: long before students begin classes they receive clear messages about the campus culture and what it means to be a member of the Gonzaga community.

- *How and by whom are prospective students socialized at your campus?*
- *When does acculturation begin and what impact does it have on student success?*
- *What programs are in place to communicate high expectations to newcomers?*
- *How do you know students "hear" the messages you intend to send?*
- *If your institution should socialize newcomers more effectively, how can you determine what needs to be done to put new initiatives in place? How will you measure their effectiveness?*

First-Year Seminar: Wheaton College

All Wheaton's first-year students take the First-Year Seminar (FYS) in the first semester of college. First-Year Seminar is a credit-bearing experience taught by a team of instructors, including a faculty member, a librarian, and two preceptors (junior- or senior-level students). The faculty member is the student's academic advisor throughout the first year, or until the student selects an academic major. The progress of FYS groups and individual students are monitored by the faculty. First-Year Seminar preceptors help facilitate the discussion sections of large introductory courses, read and evaluate student papers, assist with library training, and serve as peer mentors. Thus, FYS at Wheaton is an extended academic socialization process for new students, requiring the cooperation and contributions of many elements of the campus community.

- *What structures, events, and processes introduce new students to academic and other community expectations at your institution?*
- *What systems are in place to help new students negotiate the transition to college effectively?*
- *If your institution has a first-year seminar, to what extent is it achieving its objectives? What do students learn in the seminars? Are modifications necessary?*
- *If your institution does not have a first-year seminar program or something similar, should one be considered? What evidence supports your conclusions?*
- *If a summer, pre-school, program should be considered, what should be done to put it in place? What are the obstacles you face in developing this kind of program and how might they be overcome?*

The First Year College: Winston-Salem State University

The First Year College (FYC) and Academic Support Services division of Winston-Salem State University (WSSU) is home to all new first-year students, readmitted students, undecided students, and transfer students with fewer than 12 credit hours. The First Year College's purpose is to enhance academic performance and adjustment of students through specialized advising and support services, including counseling, monitoring, tutoring, developmental advising, computer-assisted instruction, and other learning assistance programs. Most of the offices and programs associated with the FYC are housed in one building near the center of campus, which allows support staff to work together to create supportive environments for new students. Freshman seminars are required of all students, and students who need additional academic monitoring and counseling meet with Center for Student Success (CSS) staff who, along with the faculty, monitor students' academic performance. Tutors and peer leaders, such as Campus PALs (Peer Advisor Leaders), also help mentor students and keep faculty and students informed of services available in the Center.

- *To what extent are your services and structures for new students effective?*
- *Are structures in place to identify students at risk?*
- *How well do offices, services, and people focused on your new students work together?*
- *If a comprehensive program for new students is appropriate for your campus, what would you need to do to put a trial program of this type in place? Whose support and cooperation are necessary? What obstacles would you have to overcome?*

V. Improvement-Oriented Ethos

DEEP colleges are "positively restless." Confident about what they are and where they want to go, they believe they can always improve. They monitor, in formal and informal ways, where they are, what they are doing, and whether they are making progress toward desired goals and objectives. They are open to trying new, promising approaches to teaching and learning. DEEP schools do not, however, desire to be *like* any other institution; they simply want to be the best *they* can be. They also understand that improvement efforts are pointless without relevant evidence, so they collect data about all aspects of institutional and student life and use that information to inform decisions. Supporting this orientation toward improvement is a "can-do" ethic that permeates these campuses, a system of values and beliefs that reflects the institutions' willingness to take on matters of substance consistent with their priorities and commitment to student success. Even when resources are in short supply, small amounts of money usually can be found to support mission-related initiatives that promote student success.

Chapters One, Six, Thirteen, and Fourteen of *Student Success in College* present detailed information about the improvement-oriented ethos common to DEEP institutions.

Diagnostic Queries

Openness to Innovate

1. To what extent does the institution value and foster innovation, experimentation, and risk-taking? What messages do

institutional members hear about the need for or desirability of innovation, experimentation, and risk-taking in the name of improving educational effectiveness? Is start-up money available to support innovative ideas? Are those funds used effectively? By and for whom?

2. To what extent and in what ways are people in the institution committed to ongoing institutional improvement and to enhancing student success? Is an improvement-oriented ethos widely shared, or is it concentrated in a few places or levels of the institution?

3. To what extent and in what ways do people exhibit a "can do" attitude about institutional improvement? About their work with students?

Data to Inform and Evaluate Improvement Efforts

1. What data related to student success and effective educational practice are collected, for what purposes, and by whom? How are they used?

2. To what degree do people use data to inform and evaluate decisions, policies, and practices?

3. What messages do community members hear about the importance of data for shaping day-to-day activities as well as broad policy decisions? To what extent are individuals and offices accountable for collecting and using reliable and valid data?

Resource Allocation

1. How are budget priorities and allocations determined?

2. In what ways are budget priorities and allocations consistent with the educational mission, institutional values, and student success efforts?

3. What role do students play in allocating resources?

Vignettes: Improvement-Oriented Ethos

Student Work Initiative: University of Maine at Farmington

The University of Maine at Farmington (UMF) is committed to serving students in its region, many of whom are first-generation college students. Because most UMF students must work to pay college expenses, the university decided to enhance the likelihood that work would contribute to student success and not hinder engagement, learning, and persistence. Initiated in 1998, the Student Work Initiative is a campus-based work and learn program designed to promote student-faculty and student-staff interaction and connect students to the campus in meaningful ways. Positions are funded by federal work-study, departmental budgets, and discretionary funds from the president's office. The initiative provides staffing for a variety of programs, offices, and research and teaching support for faculty. Moreover, it creates opportunities for students to interact with and learn from faculty and staff in informal settings. Students learn to apply what they are gaining in classes to practical, real-life situations. In the process, they become familiar with the world of professional work and gain insights about employment after graduation. Due in large part to the Student Work Initiative, more than half of all UMF students (1,000) have jobs on campus and the university's persistence-to-graduation rate is on the rise.

- *How many of your students engage in educationally relevant employment, on and off campus?*

- *To what extent might student employment enhance institutional effectiveness by performing needed tasks in institutional programs and offices?*

- *To what extent might faculty research and teaching be facilitated by student workers?*

- *If desirable, how might meaningful on-campus student work opportunities be expanded?*

- *How might desired learning outcomes be incorporated into students' current work experiences?*

Early Warning Systems: Fayetteville State University

The Early Alert System at Fayetteville State University (FSU) identifies and supports students at academic risk through an intricate network of faculty members, mentors, and academic support staff. All new FSU first-year students participate in University College, a comprehensive initiative designed to facilitate students' transition to college. Within the first two weeks of each semester, all faculty members teaching freshman-level courses receive a list of the mentors of the first-year students in their classes so they can contact mentors and University College staff if students experience difficulty. Students at risk receive letters about their progress from University College, which also directs students to the appropriate support service(s). Finally, Advisement and Career Services Center staff apprise students of strategies that can help them address academic and adjustment problems. In addition to providing direct services and interventions, FSU's Early Alert System sends a clear symbolic message to students: the institution values them and is committed to helping them succeed.

- *What early warning systems are in place at your institution? Whom do they serve and how well?*

- *How are students who are struggling identified?*

- *Do faculty know where or to whom to refer students experiencing difficulties?*

- *Would a complex, comprehensive support program make sense at your institution? If so, what steps would be necessary to put such a system in place? What obstacles might these efforts encounter and how might they be overcome?*

VI. Shared Responsibility for Educational Quality and Student Success

People on DEEP campuses see themselves as educators. Student learning is widely accepted as everyone's responsibility (Kinzie & Kuh, 2004). At these institutions, faculty, staff, and students enjoy mutual respect based on shared commitment to the institution's mission. Effective partnerships—particularly between faculty and student affairs professionals—reflect and support the collaborative spirit and positive attitude that characterize these campuses. In addition, every DEEP campus has one or more key leaders and senior faculty members who speak persuasively about institutional aspirations and the importance of learning-centered priorities. Through their actions and words, senior administrators and faculty model preferred ways of interacting, making decisions, and responding to challenges. Equally important, hundreds of individuals make countless small gestures on a daily basis that create and sustain a caring community for students.

DEEP schools also expect and teach students to take responsibility for their learning and that of their peers. Many students on every DEEP campus are articulate champions for their school's mission and educational programs. They influence their peers to get involved in the life of the institution.

Chapters One, Seven, Thirteen, and Fourteen of *Student Success in College* contain detailed information about how DEEP institutions have cultivated and sustain shared responsibility for student learning and success on their campuses.

Diagnostic Queries

Institutional Leadership

1. Where do students, their learning, and their success appear on the agendas of formal and informal institutional leaders? What do institutional leaders say about students and success to internal parties? To external groups?

2. What messages do institutional leaders communicate to faculty and staff including librarians, instructional technology professionals, and student affairs professionals about the importance of students and the role of faculty and staff in fostering student learning?

3. How do students, faculty, and staff describe the attitudes of institutional leaders about the importance of students? About shared responsibility for student success and educational quality?

4. How do institutional leaders model shared responsibility for student success and educational quality?

Campus Partnerships

1. To what extent and in what ways do academic affairs staff, faculty, librarians, instructional technology professionals, and their policies, programs, and practices reflect and support the educational mission of the institution?

2. To what extent and in what ways do student affairs staff and their policies, programs, and practices reflect and support: (1) the educational mission of the institution? (2) academic programs and priorities? (3) students' learning and success?

3. To what extent and in what ways do academic and student affairs offices, programs, and personnel collaborate to facilitate student success? What barriers exist to this collaboration? What factors facilitate collaboration?

4. Do other staff who have contact with students in campus offices, in maintenance roles, in food services, and in other venues see themselves as responsible for maintaining educational quality and contributing to student success?

5. To what extent and in what ways do academic affairs, student affairs, faculty, staff, administrators, and students share values and assumptions about students and their learning? To what extent and in what ways do their values and assumptions about students differ? What impact, if any, do these differences have on student success?

Student Responsibility

1. To what extent do students feel they and their success are institutional priorities?

2. What messages are communicated to students about their responsibility for the quality of their own learning and for their own success? To what extent and in what ways do students feel responsible for the quality of their peers' learning and success?

3. What roles do students play in:

   Campus governance?

   Institutional leadership and planning?

   Faculty and staff recruitment and selection?

   Student activities and governance?

   Development and/or delivery of academic support services for students?

   Socialization of new students, faculty, and staff?

   Supervision of residence life?

   Development and/or delivery of off-campus programs, including service learning?

4. How widely distributed are such roles throughout the student body? In what ways are students prepared for and supported in these roles? In what ways are students held accountable for performing these roles effectively?

Vignettes: Shared Responsibility for Learning

Structures for Systematic Collaboration: Longwood University

Longwood University students benefit from a strong, long-standing partnership between student affairs and academic affairs, blurring the boundaries and work of these units. Most Longwood faculty members are dedicated to nurturing and caring for students to an extent one typically expects from student affairs professionals. At the same time, student affairs aspires to be noted for its efforts to integrate academic and cocurricular experiences. The work of resident assistants (RAs), for example, is part of the educational mission, and RAs receive helpful training and advice for carrying out this role. Longwood also avoids the organizational and operational divisions that often exist between academic and student affairs. Because the vice president of student affairs (VPSA) reports to the provost and is a member of the Dean's Council, the VPSA is in direct and frequent communication with academic leaders and faculty. Such regular interaction helps maintain strong relationships between academic departments and the student affairs division, and has helped to bring about a high degree of faculty involvement in student affairs programs.

- *To what extent do structures at your institution facilitate or inhibit collaboration across divisional lines?*

- *Do academic and student affairs leaders have shared understandings of the institutional mission?*

- *To what extent do the activities, practices, and policies of academic and student affairs reinforce and support one another? To what extent are they contradictory?*

- *If current structures and practices hinder collaboration, what can and should be done to create collaboration?*

Seamless Learning: The Evergreen State College

True to its founding ideals and values, Evergreen State College's academic and management structures and operating philosophy are different from those at most state-supported colleges and universities. An unusual but functional egalitarianism and a noteworthy level of caring and sense of community are two Evergreen qualities that focus faculty and staff on educating the whole student. For example, student affairs staff members administer the usual variety of functions and services, including admissions, counseling, health services, student organization advising, orientation, and residence life. At the same time, personal issues that can get in the way of learning are not ignored by Evergreen faculty members and left for student affairs alone to address. In fact, Evergreen faculty members often behave in ways that resemble student affairs professionals, offering support and advice on personal issues as well as academic matters. For their part, student affairs staff contribute in integral ways to "teaching across significant differences," one of five priorities emphasized in the college's mission. In short, traditional notions of "academic affairs" and "student affairs" and the boundaries and territories that can define the two have no meaning at Evergreen; instead of thinking of the lines between student affairs and faculty as blurred, few, if any, lines exist.

- *To what extent are boundaries and lines between academic and student affairs visible or invisible at your institution? What impact does this have on students and their learning and other aspects of institutional effectiveness?*

- *If developing a collaborative ethic at your institution is desirable, how might faculty and student affairs staff work together to make this happen? What problems and obstacles would need to be addressed for such an effort to succeed?*

"Ultimately, It's About the Culture"

By now, it should be clear that student success is in part a function of complicated, inextricably intertwined institutional factors and conditions—educational mission, operating philosophies, resources, programs, and practices to name few. We conclude this section of ISES by focusing on what holds these various properties together: institutional culture.

Culture is the tie that binds, the "invisible tapestry" (Kuh & Whitt, 1988) that connects and gives meaning to activities and events. Norms, values, and tacit assumptions and beliefs about students work together to provide a purpose and direction for community members and their activities and highlight institutional priorities. Thus, as with so many aspects of institutional effectiveness, the whole of the cultural properties that comprise and contribute to student success is greater than the sum of the parts. Principle Two in Chapter Two notes that individual practices cannot be separated from their context, and each aspect of effectiveness—mission, focus on student learning, pathways to success, and so on—reflects and is reflected in the others.

The cultures of individual DEEP schools are, of course, not without contested terrain. Each struggles to varying degrees with inconsistencies and lack of consensus about critical issues; diverse and sometimes competing perspectives exist about the institution's current priorities and aspirations. Such differences—at DEEP institutions or at any other college or university—should not be viewed necessarily as shortcomings or as evidence of a dysfunctional culture (Kuh, Schuh, Whitt, & Associates, 1991; Martin, 2002). What is notable about the cultures and subcultures of DEEP schools, however, is the centrality of student success in their missions and the extent to which they consistently communicate this priority.

Chapters One, Two, Thirteen, and Fourteen of *Student Success in College* present additional detailed information about the cultural properties at DEEP institutions that value, promote, and support student success. As you think about examining and understanding the cultures and subcultures (including student cultures) of your institution, consider focusing on: artifacts (such as rituals, traditions, stories, myths, ceremonies, language, norms), values, or widely held beliefs about who can learn what here and who cannot, who deserves an education and who does not, and the importance of certain goals, activities, and relationships (Kuh & Whitt, 1988).

Diagnostic Queries

Institutional Cultures

1. What is special about this institution? What is special to students? What is special to faculty? What is special to staff? How do these distinctive aspects of the institution affect the campus climate? How do these special aspects of the institution affect student success?

2. What do institutional leaders communicate through their words and deeds about the importance of students and their learning?

3. In what ways do the institutional culture and the dominant subcultures of the institution promote or inhibit student learning and success?

4. How do the following influence student success:

    Language that administrators, faculty, and others use to communicate the relative importance of students and their learning?

    Language that includes some students and excludes others, or privileges certain groups over others, and the impact on student success?

    Symbols and symbolic actions that communicate the relative importance of various groups of students and their learning?

    Messages and cultural values that are embedded in cultural artifacts, such as orientation activities, institutional ceremonies, and institutional rituals?

Student Cultures

1. How do students describe what they learn, how they learn, and from whom? In what ways are students' experiences consistent and inconsistent with those desired and/or claimed by the institution?

2. In what ways do the student culture and/or dominant student subcultures promote student learning and success? In what ways do the student culture and/or dominant student subcultures inhibit student learning and success?

3. What opportunities exist to celebrate students and their learning? What opportunities exist to celebrate institutional values? What opportunities exist to celebrate the campus community? What role do students play in these celebrations?

4. How do the following cultural influences affect student success:

The language students use to talk about how the institution treats them and the extent to which it values their learning?

The languages of student cultures that reinforce or contradict the educational values of the institution?

The symbols and symbolic actions of student cultures that communicate the educational values of the institution?

The messages and cultural values communicated by cultural artifacts, such student traditions, heroes and heroines, rituals, and legends?

Vignettes: Institutional and Student Cultures

Educating Men: Wabash College

Wabash College has been educating men for more than 170 years. Student engagement is in large part a function of the institution's strong, coherent campus culture and its mission, which is conveyed in a single sentence: "Wabash College educates men to think critically, act responsibly, lead effectively, and live humanely." From their initial contacts with the college, prospective students are told that a Wabash education is challenging, but, as the admissions materials say, "it's worth it." The college subscribes to five core values: (1) a rigorous liberal arts education; (2) personalized teaching and learning; (3) individual responsibility and trust; (4) a socially, economically, and ethnically diverse student body; and (5) a tradition and philosophy of independence. These five key elements are prominent in all aspects of college life, from admissions brochures and freshman orientation activities, to long-range planning, resource allocation decisions, and policymaking. High expectations, a rigorous liberal arts curriculum, a challenging and supportive faculty, a cocurriculum rooted in individual responsibility and trust, common academic experiences, meaningful traditions, and a diverse student body encourage students to assume responsibility for creating and directing their education.

- *To what extent is your school's culture clear, coherent, and strong?*
- *Does the culture of your institution enhance or hinder student success?*
- *In what ways are the artifacts, values, and beliefs of the dominant student culture and student subcultures consistent with or contradictory to the educational goals of the institution?*
- *What elements of the institutional and/or student cultures should be preserved or changed to achieve more consistency with the educational mission? How might this change occur?*

Engagement from the Ground Up:
California State University at Monterey Bay

During its short history, California State University at Monterey Bay (CSUMB) has developed a strong, coherent culture that values student development and success. Founded in 1994, CSUMB organizes its academic programs according to innovative, learner-centered principles of interdisciplinary and outcomes-based education. Today, the university is marked by interdisciplinary academic programs, active and collaborative learning, and service learning integrated into the curriculum. The pioneering zeal of the founding CSUMB faculty pushed the development of effective educational programs and fostered a strong sense of ownership for the institution. Institutional leaders model the institution's values and aspiration to provide a distinctive, high-quality undergraduate education. By recruiting faculty and staff members who are willing to experiment, the campus is inclined to innovate without facing significant resistance. Its outcomes-based education (OBE) model places student learning at the center of the institution, replacing the all-too-familiar credit hours and seat time as measures of learning with systematic assessments of authentic student learning. By employing active and collaborative learning approaches and accepting many types of evidence to fulfill a particular learning outcome, faculty members acknowledge that different students have different strengths and learning styles. All students must complete two service learning experiences, one at the lower division of the curriculum and one at the upper division. This requirement reinforces the expectation that CSUMB students will act on what they learn.

- *How does your institution cultivate a coherent culture that values students and their success?*

- *To what extent do cultural properties support or inhibit enactment of your institution's espoused mission?*

- *Should some elements of the culture be modified to promote experimentation with promising pedagogical approaches or more consistent use of effective educational practices? How might this be done?*

CHAPTER 4

Using ISES to Assess Effective Educational Practices

This chapter presents the second half of the Inventory and focuses on the five clusters of effective educational practice featured on the National Survey of Student Engagement (NSSE). Commonly known as benchmarks, the NSSE clusters are conceptual categories that capture many important student behaviors and institutional factors related to desired outcomes of college. The clusters are

- Academic challenge
- Active and collaborative learning
- Student-faculty interaction
- Enriching educational experiences
- Supportive campus environment

Taken together, these factors and conditions contribute to student satisfaction and achievement on a variety of dimensions. Questions in this section can help you reflect on the promising practices of DEEP schools in the context of your institutional culture. You might also want to develop additional questions that are meaningful for your setting. In addition, if your institution participates in NSSE, your benchmark data could help you pinpoint areas for further exploration using the diagnostic queries.

Many of the effective practices we described in *Student Success in College* (Kuh et al., 2005) and in the following sections of the Inventory are familiar to most readers. Learning communities, first-year seminars, service learning, and study abroad opportunities have proliferated in recent years. Recall, however, three factors that distinguish DEEP schools: (1) the high quality of their programs and practices, (2) the large numbers of students who are touched in meaningful ways by these initiatives, and (3) the institutions' commitment to ongoing assessment to determine what activities are necessary and appropriate in their contexts and for their students and what activities to avoid or discontinue. These factors work together to enhance student engagement and persistence at levels beyond what might be expected.

The policies, programs, and practices at DEEP colleges and universities represent possibilities to consider. Your school's decision to adopt or adapt one or more depends on many factors, including the effectiveness of existing policies and practices, student characteristics, and other relevant features of your campus context. Answering the following questions can help you sift through priorities for taking action:

- Do we do this? How well do we do this? How do we know?

- How many students do related initiatives touch in meaningful ways and what is our evidence for this? Whom do we fail to reach? What might we do to reach them?

- To what extent do our programs, policies, and practices reflect and support the educational mission and values of the institution?

- To what extent are our programs and practices complementary and synergistic? To what extent are they fragmented or hit-and-miss? To what extent do they compete with one another and/or the institution's educational purposes?

- Can our financial and human resources sustain our educationally effective programs?

- What are we doing that is *not* represented among the policies and practices described here and what evidence justifies doing it?

- What could we stop without negative consequences? What must we continue and what evidence supports that decision?

- What are we not doing that we should? How might we adapt certain policies and practices for our unique institutional culture and circumstances?

- To what extent do we use systematic evidence—from outcomes assessment, program evaluations, current research on educational effectiveness—to review and determine our policies, practices, and programs?

- What promising educational practices should be considered in addition to those represented on the NSSE survey and described in *Student Success in College*?

Academic Challenge

Challenging intellectual and creative work is central to student learning and high-quality collegiate experiences. Colleges and universities promote high levels of student achievement by setting high expectations for student performance and holding students accountable for performing at such levels.

Academic challenge represents the amount of time and effort students devote to (1) studying and other academic work, (2) preparing for class, (3) reading assigned and other books, and (4) writing reports and papers. Academic challenge also addresses the extent to which students engage in activities that require analyzing, synthesizing, applying theories, and making judgments, as well as the extent to which instructors set standards that compel students to work harder than they thought possible. DEEP schools promote high levels of academic challenge by setting and holding students to high expectations and by providing appropriate levels of support. Efforts to acculturate students to the values of the academy and to channel student energy toward educationally productive activities inside and outside classrooms sustain this ethos. Most DEEP institutions, for example, emphasize writing across the curriculum and provide rigorous culminating experiences for seniors. Most also require that students employ higher-order thinking skills to complete assignments and class projects. Finally, they also celebrate student and faculty achievement publicly.

Chapters One, Eight, and Fourteen of *Student Success in College* offer examples of how DEEP colleges and universities present academic challenges to their students.

Diagnostic Queries

High Expectations

In what ways and to what extent:

1. Are expectations for student performance set at appropriately high levels, given students' academic preparation?

2. Are expectations for student performance clearly and consistently articulated?

3. Are students performing at the desired levels?

4. Are rigorous, integrative, culminating experiences expected of seniors?

5. Are academic challenges for students balanced by appropriate support?

6. Are student achievement and academic performance valued and celebrated publicly?

7. Are students expected, and taught, to assess their learning needs and seek assistance when they need it?

8. Does the campus climate emphasize academic achievement and intellectual curiosity? Free expression of ideas? Self-discovery? Collaboration on academic work?

9. Do opportunities and settings for out-of-class involvement (student leadership, campus residences, student organizations) support and encourage, or inhibit, rigorous academic expectations?

Rigorous Academic Work

In what ways and to what extent:

1. Do students have to stretch to meet academic standards and expectations?

2. Do faculty members assess students' prior knowledge and competencies and design—or allow students to design—assignments to progress from where they are to where they need to go?

3. Do students devote time and energy to preparing for classes? Is student time on task consistent with faculty expectations and course demands? If not, why?

4. Do classes emphasize higher-order cognitive and intellectual activities?

5. Do students engage in extensive and intensive writing, reading, and class preparation?

6. Are examinations and class assignments challenging? Does the level of challenge differ by year in school, lower- and upper-division courses, and majors? Are the differences understandable and acceptable?

7. Does student performance vary across years in school, lower- and upper-division course, and major? Are the variations understandable and acceptable?

8. Does student performance differ by student group (part-time students, student athletes, students of color, members of sororities and fraternities, off-campus residents)? Are the differences understandable and acceptable?

Vignettes: Academic Challenge

Organizing the First Year Around Ideas:
Ursinus College's Common Intellectual Experience

While preparing for a Middle States Accreditation visit in the late 1990s, Ursinus College faculty members decided to modify the curriculum in ways that would raise the level of intellectual discourse on campus, bring coherence to the first year of study, and help students move from dependent or guided learning to independent learning. From these deliberations came the Common Intellectual Experience (CIE), which is now required of all first-year students. CIE is interdisciplinary in orientation and exposes students to a wide range of challenging readings on complex philosophical topics from original texts and writing assignments that address such daunting questions as "What does it mean to be human?" Student achievement is celebrated publicly by displaying student artwork and research presentations in college publications. Although some first-year students have mixed feelings about the course, upper-division students reported the CIE prepared them well for the rest of their time at the college, especially by helping to hone critical thinking and writing skills.

- *How have accreditation self-studies or other reviews influenced undergraduate programs at your school? How might you take advantage of such opportunities in the future?*

- *What would be required to motivate your faculty colleagues to examine and redesign—if warranted—the curriculum to enhance intellectual vitality and bring greater coherence to students' learning experiences?*

Writing Across the Curriculum: George Mason University

Begun through the efforts of a faculty task force in the late 1970s, George Mason University's (GMU) writing across the curriculum initiative is credited with creating and sustaining a focus on rigor and excellence across majors and courses. Initial funding for the initiative came from the Northern Virginia Writing Project; subsequent support has been provided by grants from the Commonwealth and the university. A recent edition of *US News & World Report* placed GMU fourth in the writing in the disciplines category; Harvard, Cornell, Yale, and Princeton rounded out the top five positions. Since 1995, every GMU student has been required to take freshman composition, advanced composition, and at least one writing-intensive course in the major. Some writing-intensive courses require writing portfolios (for example, nursing) or design projects (for example, engineering). In some majors, such as public and international affairs, every course at the 300-level and above is a writing-intensive course. The result? Students think more critically and work harder. They also learn their ideas are taken seriously.

- *To what extent is writing across the curriculum featured on your campus? To what extent is this approach effective?*

- *In what majors or areas do students write more and benefit more from their writing than others?*

- *What would it take to make writing and the intellectual skills and attitudes allied with writing more important, visible, and practiced at your school?*

Continuous Feedback: Sweet Briar College

Ongoing, substantive feedback on academic performance is a way of life at Sweet Briar where faculty members engage students in a cycle of continuous feedback and improvement. Often, students receive one or more pages of typed notes with an assignment noting how it can be improved. The feedback is very direct and delivered in a matter-of-fact way that reinforces the high expectations faculty members have for student performance. This pedagogical practice creates an environment where students can learn and improve; it is part of the culture of Sweet Briar College.

- *To what extent and in what ways is timely, continuous feedback to students an important pedagogical practice at your institution?*

- *What means for feedback are used, such as written comments, oral critiques of work, and juries or external reviews? To what extent are any or all of these strategies effective?*

- *If feedback does not occur to the extent it should, how might its use be increased?*

Active and Collaborative Learning

Students learn when they are intensely involved in their education and have opportunities to think about and apply what they are learning in different settings. Furthermore, when students collaborate with others to solve problems and master difficult material, they acquire valuable skills to address situations and problems they encounter during and after college.

DEEP schools employ a variety of active and collaborative learning strategies to accommodate diverse learning styles and involve students in their learning. As a result, students can apply what they learn to practical problems and take advantage of learning opportunities that prepare them to work effectively in groups. Included among the effective active and collaborative learning practices at DEEP institutions are those on the NSSE survey: (1) asking questions in class and/or contributing to class discussions; (2) making class presentations; (3) working with other students on class projects inside or outside of class; (4) tutoring other students; (5) participating in a community-based project as part of a course; and (6) discussing ideas from readings or classes with other students, family members, or others outside of class.

Chapters One, Nine, Thirteen, and Fourteen of *Student Success in College* provide detailed information and numerous examples of active and collaborative learning approaches used at DEEP institutions.

Diagnostic Queries

Active Learning

In what ways and to what extent:

1. Is active learning expected and practiced throughout the undergraduate curriculum?

2. Are students instructed how to participate actively in class?

3. Are engaging pedagogies used in classes of all sizes and in different areas of the curriculum, such as lower- and upper-division courses and across major fields? If differences in use exist, are they based on evidence related to student learning and success?

4. Do students ask questions in class and actively participate in class discussion?

5. Do electronic technologies foster active learning?

6. Are internships, community work, service learning, and other activities that allow students to use and practice what they are learning widely distributed across the student body?

7. Do cocurricular activities and organizations expect and encourage students to use and practice out of class what they are learning in class?

Collaborative Learning

In what ways and to what extent:

1. Is collaborative learning expected and implemented throughout the undergraduate curriculum?

2. Are students taught how to learn collaboratively?

3. Do faculty model collaboration across disciplines and organizational units?

4. Are collaborative learning and problem-solving activities used in classes and elsewhere on campus?

5. Are group study and other forms of collaboration encouraged by physical and curricular structures?

6. Do electronic technologies foster collaborative learning?

7. Do peers mentor and teach peers, paid or volunteer, with or without academic credit?

8. Are peer evaluation and feedback expected and taught? Do students provide feedback to their peers?

Learning Communities

In what ways and to what extent:

1. Is the surrounding community used as an extended classroom?

2. Are residential and nonresidential learning communities available to address a wide variety of student needs and interests? Are these communities effective in fostering student learning and success?

3. Do students seek membership in and benefit from residential and nonresidential learning communities?

4. Do residential and nonresidential learning communities facilitate collaborative learning for students and faculty?

Vignettes: Active and Collaborative Learning

Accountability for Learning: California State University at Monterey Bay

Active and collaborative learning approaches are featured at California State University at Monterey Bay (CSUMB) in the structures used to hold students accountable for their learning. For example, students involved in group projects evaluate one another, and faculty provide individual as well as group grades on assignments. Small groups present their work to their entire class. Furthermore, in-class group assignments are highly structured. When organizing work groups, for example, faculty assign a person to take notes and a person to keep the group on task. Such practices are routine across courses and require that students take an additional measure of responsibility for their own learning as well as that of their peers.

- *To what extent are active and collaborative learning activities used in undergraduate courses at your institution?*
- *Would more (or less) active and collaborative learning be desirable? Why or why not? If more would be better, how might that happen? What obstacles would have to be overcome?*

Peer Tutoring: The University of Texas at El Paso

More than 70% of University of Texas at El Paso (UTEP) seniors have tutored or taught other students at some point during college, well above the national average of 56%. Moreover, becoming a tutor at UTEP is serious business. Students who work at the Tutoring Learning Center (TLC) must have minimum cumulative and major grade point averages of 3.0 and strong letters of recommendation from two faculty members. In addition, they must be certified by the College Reading and Learning Association. Once hired, student tutors must complete formal training (paid for by the institution), maintain a 3.0 grade point average in all coursework and the major, and tutor a prescribed number of hours each week. Tutors benefit in several ways from their experiences: application of principles learned in class, enhanced communication and leadership skills, active engagement in academic pursuits, meaningful interaction with faculty, and experience as peer mentors.

- *How common is peer tutoring—formal and informal—at your institution?*
- *Does your institution provide structures to encourage and enhance peer tutoring?*
- *To what extent and in what ways do students use the services of peer tutors?*
- *Should more peer tutoring be available at your institution? If so, what would need to be in place to make this happen? Could current resources be organized to support more tutoring on your campus?*

Student-Faculty Interaction_____

Students learn firsthand to think about and solve practical problems by interacting with faculty members inside and outside of classrooms. Through interactions with students, faculty become role models, mentors, and guides for continuous, lifelong learning.

Meaningful, substantive interactions between students and their teachers are essential to high-quality learning experiences. DEEP schools fashion policies and programs to encourage such interactions. The types of contacts students have with faculty measured by the NSSE survey are: (1) talking about career plans with a faculty member or advisor; (2) discussing ideas from readings or classes with faculty members outside of class; (3) receiving prompt feedback from faculty on academic performance; (4) working with a faculty member on a research project; (5) working with faculty members on activities other than coursework (committees, orientation, student-life activities, and so on); and (6) discussing grades or assignments with an instructor.

Faculty at DEEP colleges and universities are accessible and responsive to students' needs, both in and out of the classroom. They provide timely and extensive feedback, collaborate frequently with students on research and scholarly projects, and generally subscribe to a holistic philosophy of student development. Finally, faculty members experiment with electronic technologies to facilitate and enrich interactions between and among students, faculty, and staff.

Chapters One, Ten, Thirteen, and Fourteen of *Student Success in College* provide examples of student-faculty interactions at DEEP schools.

Diagnostic Queries

Student-Faculty Collaboration

In what ways and to what extent:

1. Do faculty members meet with students outside of class for course-related and non-course-related purposes, such as discussing assignments or talking about career plans?

2. Do faculty and students work together on campus committees and in other ways outside the classroom?

3. Do faculty members collaborate on research with undergraduates?

4. Are opportunities to collaborate with faculty distributed widely across the student body?

5. Can students get two or more faculty members to write meaningful letters of reference to support applications for employment, graduate school, or for other reasons?

Student-Centered Activities

In what ways and to what extent:

1. Are faculty and other staff, such as librarians, student affairs professionals, academic advisors, and instructional technology personnel recruited, selected, and prepared to engage with students and their learning?

2. Are faculty and staff accessible (in both the physical and psychological meanings of the word) to students?

3. Are faculty and staff rewarded for working with undergraduates, inside and outside the classroom?

4. Do students interact with faculty face-to-face and through other modes, such as e-mail or telephone?

5. Do faculty members know students' names?

6. Do faculty members make time for students beyond posted office hours?

7. Do students receive extensive and timely feedback from faculty?

8. Do students find faculty helpful and responsive? Are students satisfied with the quality of their relationships with faculty and staff? Is the institution satisfied with the quality of student-faculty and student-staff relationships?

9. Do campus structures and facilities foster interactions among community members, including between students and faculty?

Vignettes: Student-Faculty Interaction

Students as Colleagues: Macalester College

Extensive and intensive interactions between Macalester students and faculty begin early. All first-year students take First Year Seminars (FYS) and their FYS instructor serves as their advisor. Because of the FYS instructor's dual role as seminar leader and advisor, faculty learn firsthand about their advisees' intellectual interests and strengths and limitations. Moreover, they see their advisees several times a week, which provides frequent opportunities for informal conversations and useful information about academic and social adjustment. Macalester's Campus Center provides space for faculty, staff, and students to eat together in the café, and faculty are reimbursed for meals taken there with students. Students also serve on hiring and tenure committees alongside faculty; many work on research projects with faculty, something strongly encouraged by academic administrators. For example, the provost asks his colleagues routinely, "How does your research with students enrich their experience?" Much collaborative research takes place during the summer with financial support that enables teams of faculty and students to work together for four to ten weeks.

- *In what ways does your institution encourage and support meaningful interactions between students and faculty?*

> ▪ *What is the nature of interactions and relationships between students and faculty at your college?*
>
> ▪ *How are meaningful student-faculty relationships supported or inhibited?*
>
> ▪ *What would need to happen to enhance student-faculty interactions and relationships at your institution?*

Creating Opportunities for Student-Faculty Interaction: University of Kansas

The University of Kansas has a long history of encouraging student-faculty interactions. Since the 1950s, the institution has provided funds to support undergraduate research with faculty. Today, faculty and students come together each spring to implement the Undergraduate Research Symposium, a Saturday devoted to student presentations of original research and other creative activities. Another long-standing practice that fuels student-faculty interaction is the requirement that students comprise at least 20% of the membership of all nonpersonnel campus committees; moreover, a student serves as the vice chair of each campus committee and presides in the absence of the faculty chair.

> ▪ *Assuming it is desirable to do so, what would have to happen to increase the frequency and quality of student-faculty interaction at your institution?*
>
> ▪ *What role do faculty-student interactions play in learning outside the classroom for your students?*

Enriching Educational Experiences

> *Complementary learning opportunities inside and outside the classroom augment the academic program. Experiencing diversity teaches students valuable lessons about themselves and other cultures. Used appropriately, computer technologies facilitate learning and promote collaboration between and among students and instructors. Internships, community service, and senior capstone courses provide opportunities for students to synthesize, integrate, and apply their knowledge. Such experiences make learning more meaningful and, ultimately, more useful because what students know becomes a part of who they are.*

DEEP schools present students with an array of learning opportunities that complement and supplement their academic programs. Enriching educational experiences on the NSSE survey are: (1) having serious conversations with students of a different race or ethnicity than one's own; (2) having serious conversations with students with different religious beliefs, political opinions, and values; (3) using electronic technology to discuss or complete assignments; (4) participating in internships or field experiences, foreign language study, study abroad, community service, independent study, a culminating senior experience; (5) participating in cocurricular activities; and (6) an institutional climate that encourages contact among students from different economic, social, and racial or ethnic backgrounds.

Most DEEP institutions feature a wide variety of options for enhancing student learning through enriching educational experiences. These include perspectives on diversity infused throughout the curriculum and cocurriculum; student participation in cross-cultural learning experiences; student-centered use of computer technologies; and programs that connect students in meaningful ways with communities near and far and in the United States as well as abroad, and that prompt students to apply in the real world what they learn in classes.

Chapters One, Eleven, Thirteen, and Fourteen of *Student Success in College* illustrate the variety of ways DEEP colleges and universities enrich the educational experiences of their students.

Diagnostic Queries

Infusion of Diversity Experiences

In what ways and to what extent:

1. Are diversity experiences infused in the curriculum and cocurriculum? What are the nature and quality of students' experiences with diversity?

2. Are cross-cultural experiences linked to the curriculum and cocurriculum?

3. Do students learn the educational value of diversity as newcomers?

4. Do students' experiences with diversity continue throughout their time in college?

5. Are institutional commitments to diversity reinforced by campus physical environments?

6. Are students required to participate in courses and/or activities that promote cross-cultural understanding? Is time for self-reflection included in these activities?

Experiential Learning and Engagement

In what ways and to what extent:

1. Are students required to participate in courses and/or activities that promote civic engagement? Is time for self-reflection included in these activities?

2. Do students have ready access to service learning opportunities? Do enough students take advantage of these opportunities?

3. Are students involved in community work that is related or unrelated to their coursework? Is civic engagement integrated into the curriculum and cocurriculum?

4. Does experiential learning occur inside and outside classrooms?

5. Are students required to participate in internships, practica, and field placements? Are these experiences effective?

6. Are study abroad opportunities of varying lengths available? Do students take advantage of these opportunities? Are these opportunities educationally purposeful?

7. Do electronic technologies connect students with their peers and with faculty members in substantive, meaningful ways?

8. Do administrators support and provide resources that encourage experimentation with electronic technologies?

Cocurricular Experiences

In what ways and to what extent:

1. Are students expected and encouraged to get involved in cocurricular activities? Do students seek such involvement and with what impact on success?

2. Are cocurricular leadership experiences available? Are these experiences widely distributed among the student body?

3. Do cocurricular experiences enrich student learning?

4. Do students take advantage of cocurricular leadership experiences?

5. Are formal opportunities to develop leadership skills available? Do students take advantage of these opportunities? And how are these experiences related to student learning, satisfaction, and persistence?

Vignettes: Enriching Educational Experiences

Undergraduate Research: Wheaton College

The walls in the Wheaton College science building are covered with posters from research paper presentations based on student-faculty collaborations. These remnants of the annual fall research fair send a very powerful signal to students that the college values such work. Further, the college's Web site contains a page for student-faculty research connected to its main academics page; the research site includes a short description of past projects, current research teams in search of student members, and events that foster student-faculty research. The Web site also describes the Wheaton Research Partnership, a program through which faculty can use work-study funds to hire research assistants. Students in these roles perform a variety of tasks, including entering data, conducting library searches, reading and discussing articles, collecting data, and refining measurement instruments, all of which put them in frequent, meaningful contact with faculty.

- *To what extent are undergraduate students at your institution engaged in research with faculty?*

- *In what ways do these collaborations influence student learning?*

- *If student-faculty research projects are not common at your institution, what approaches could you take to develop or expand undergraduate research?*

Learning Through Living: Longwood University

Campus residences are central, not ancillary, to achieving Longwood's educational purposes. As with all the other student affairs programs at Longwood, residence life is organized in order to foster student development and support the Longwood mission. New students are assigned to residences according to majors, including "undecided," and many educational programs related to student interests are offered within the dorms. Undergraduate resident assistants share responsibility for involving first-year students in campus life and plan a wide range of activities to get students out of their halls and into the community.

- *To what extent are residence halls central or ancillary to the educational mission of your institution?*

- *Do residence life staff engage in programs and activities that support the educational mission, or do their priorities for students compete with that mission?*

- *Would a more central role for the residence halls in fostering learning out of class be desirable? How could this be created? What resources would be necessary for this to happen? What obstacles exist and how might they be overcome?*

"Comping": Sewanee: The University of the South

Early in their Sewanee experience, students learn about and begin to look forward to "comps"—comprehensive exams taken in the major during the senior year. The exam is an important culminating sequence of activities that requires students to apply and reflect upon the skills and knowledge they acquired during college. Comps also are an important milestone in the Sewanee experience. After completing the exams, seniors with cars discover their windows covered with witticisms relating to their major. Thus, comps are both a source of motivation to persist and a symbolic rite of closure, signaling completing one stage and beginning the next.

- *What culminating experiences are available for your students to synthesize and integrate their learning?*

- *How many students have such an experience and to what extent are they effective? How do you know?*

- *If your senior-level students do not engage in experiences that provide for the integration and application of their academic work, should they? What steps might be taken to implement such experiences? What obstacles might you face and how can they be overcome?*

Supportive Campus Environments

Students perform better and are more satisfied at colleges that are committed to their success and cultivate positive working and social relations among different groups on campus than at colleges that do not.

Supportive campus environments do not exist in a vacuum or independent of other policies and practices. The properties of a supportive campus environment complement the institution's mission, are responsive to the characteristics and needs of the student body, and are situated in a complex network of cultural assumptions, beliefs, values, norms and perceptions. NSSE survey items that reflect conditions for supportive campus environments are: (1) an institutional emphasis on providing students the support they need for academic and social success; (2) positive working and social relationships among different groups, (3) helping students cope with their nonacademic responsibilities; and (4) high-quality student relationships with other students, faculty, and the institution's administrative personnel.

DEEP institutions employ a variety of approaches to support their students, all of which are grounded in an ethic of care. Support programs and services provide resources to those who need them *when* they need them and create conditions that encourage students to take advantage of them. In addition, relationships among students, faculty, and administrators are cordial and helpful. DEEP schools convey to all their students the sense that "because you are a student here, you are capable of learning anything." A variety of services are tailored to students with specific needs. Supportive programs and practices at DEEP schools include transition programs, advising networks, peer support, safety nets, special student support initiatives, and educationally purposeful living environments.

Chapters One, Twelve, Thirteen, and Fourteen of *Student Success in College* contain detailed information about what DEEP campuses do to create and maintain supportive environments for various groups of students.

Diagnostic Queries

Transition Programs

In what ways and to what extent:

1. Do transition programs welcome and affirm newcomers?

2. Are programs available to assist in transitions to college, to employment, or to graduate school? Do students take advantage of these programs?

3. Are first-year students expected to participate in educationally purposeful programs focused on adjustment to college?

Support Programs

In what ways and to what extent:

1. Are early warning systems available and effectively identifying and responding to students at risk of failure or dropping out?

2. Are multiple safety nets of personnel and structures available *and* used by various groups of students?

3. Do early warning systems and safety nets work better for some students than others? If so, what can be done to increase their effectiveness for all students?

4. Are advising networks coordinated to respond effectively to the academic needs of students?

5. Do advising systems assist students in navigating institutional policies and practices successfully?

6. Are learning support resources available to and used by students? Are these resources effective?

Supportive Environments

In what ways and to what extent:

1. Do students provide academic and social support to their peers?

2. Are students trained to work with their peers as tutors and mentors?

3. Do residential living environments provide academic and social support?

4. Do students view faculty members as available, helpful, and sympathetic?

5. Do students view the campus administration as helpful and considerate?

6. Do students view their peers as friendly and supportive?

7. Are students satisfied with their overall college experience?

Vignettes: Supportive Campus Environment

Academic Advising for Life: Alverno College

To graduate, every Alverno College student must be proficient in the eight "abilities" or outcome domains the institution considers foundational to the liberal arts: communication, analysis, problem solving, values-based decision making, social interaction, global perspectives, effective citizenship, and aesthetic engagement. Each ability is conceptualized as a series of developmental levels corresponding to a student's progress across her college career. The student moves from general education (levels one through four) to specialized work in the major and supporting areas of study (levels five and six). Strong, active advising is essential to support the complexities of the Alverno curriculum and to ensure that students have positive mentoring, accurate information, and thoughtful direction. Advisors know their work must be consistent with and supportive of faculty expectations about the overall Alverno experience. Advisors also serve as front-line interpreters of the curriculum on behalf of the faculty. For first-year students, peer advisors work alongside a professional support staff member to forge relationships with students during New Student Orientation. The staff advisor works with the student for two years; once the student enters specialized work in her major, however, she is assigned a faculty advisor.

- *To what extent is advising at your institution viewed by students, faculty, and others as effective and supportive?*

- *In what ways and to what extent do students at your institution feel supported?*

- *If greater levels of support are desirable, how might they be implemented and by whom? What resources would have to be in place for this to occur?*

Caring for the Whole Student: Fayetteville State University

An ethos of concern, nurturance, and support for student success permeates all facets of institutional life at Fayetteville State University (FSU). The cultural messages to students and everyone else is clear: students matter and extra effort in their support is the norm. For example, faculty and staff follow up with students who miss classes, experience academic difficulty, or seem to be struggling to succeed. One FSU student described contacting a student affairs professional for help on a personal matter. Realizing the issue was beyond her sphere of responsibility, the staff person helped the student make an appointment with another office. A day later she called the student to see if the appointment was kept. One seasoned FSU administrator told DEEP site visitors that the concern for nurturing students ranges from "office assistant to custodian to top management . . . everyone has a role." Another administrator suggested, "Secretaries see themselves as an extension of advisement."

- *To what extent and in what ways do students at your institution receive the support they need to be successful?*

- *Do students who need support receive it? How do you know? If they don't, what would need to be done to make this happen?*

- *What resources are needed to provide the support students need to achieve their educational objectives? How should these resources be obtained, organized, and allocated to provide the support students need to survive and thrive in college?*

CHAPTER 5

Using ISES for Institutional Improvement

This chapter addresses logistical issues for using ISES and suggests ways information from ISES and *Student Success in College* (Kuh et al., 2005) can be used to support institutional improvement efforts. Though they are by no means exhaustive, the examples illustrate how systematically examining the factors and conditions associated with student success on your campus can inform ongoing activities, such as resource allocation and strategic planning, as well as occasional efforts, such as accreditation self-studies.

Logistical Issues

In addition to the readiness suggestions offered in Chapter Two, several other issues related to using ISES might be relevant to your context. In the following sections we describe challenges associated with initiating ISES, including developing a realistic timeline for the work, determining the needed human and financial resources (including external consultants), and deciding how to disseminate and use the results.

Preparing to Launch the ISES Process

A strategy is necessary to introduce the ISES process to relevant parties, whether that is the entire campus community, an academic unit, or an administrative division. If an accreditation review is pending, for example, ISES could guide the self-study, a topic to which we return later. The appointment of a new senior leadership team could be a propitious time to take stock of institutional conditions for student learning, providing a "fresh" look at the state of affairs and generating a data-informed agenda for prioritizing improvement efforts. ISES can also be a framework for evaluating the impact of existing initiatives, such as activities related to scholarship of teaching and learning, diversity, and first-year experience.

Whatever the rationale for using ISES, unequivocal public support by key institutional leaders is essential. The president, senior academic and student life officers, and faculty and student governance bodies should endorse the process, actively engage and contribute to it, and be committed to taking appropriate action on the findings.

Timeline

Determining precisely the amount of time needed to implement an institutionwide application of ISES is difficult because many variables come into play. These include the scope of the project, availability of necessary information, and unforeseen complications. As a general rule, you can anticipate that an institutionwide ISES project will take about an academic year from start to finish, as illustrated in Table 5.1. Of course, putting the results to use will take much longer, and, to be most effective, the self-examination processes inherent in ISES should never really end.

Table 5.1   Institutionwide ISES Process Timeline

Dates	Task
Months 1 & 2	Define purpose and scope of study and outline project goals.
	Convene ISES steering committee.
	Review and refine project purpose(s) and scope.
	Identify and acquire human and fiscal resources necessary for the project.
	Announce the ISES initiative and articulate goals to key members of the campus community to cultivate commitment to engaging in the process and using the results.
	Determine approach to gathering data (e.g., involvement of internal personnel only, use of external consultants) and inquiry methods (e.g., quantitative instruments, such as NSSE or CSEQ, qualitative methods).
	Identify and assign planning team roles and responsibilities, including project leadership, participant training, and quality control.
	Coordinate project in consideration of other institutional research and assessment priorities.

Table 5.1 Institutionwide ISES Process Timeline, Cont'd

Dates	Task
	Identify members of the ISES study team (including external consultants if appropriate).
	Secure Human Subjects/Institutional Review Committee approval.
	Obtain or develop data collection tools.
Months 3 & 4	Hold ISES study team training and orientation sessions.
	Refine research approach for ISES (e.g., interviews, case study method, action research).
	Identify all potential data sources. Invite study participants.
	Develop observation, interview, and focus group protocols.
	Determine approaches for recording and storing data.
	Obtain data collection aids (e.g., tape recorders, tapes).
	Administer quantitative instruments and arrange for analysis and interpretation.
	Review documents, prepare for study.
	Arrange schedule and locations for interviews and meetings.
	Begin collecting interview and observation data.
Months 5 & 6	Continue collecting interview and observation data.
	Begin analyzing initial interview and observation data.
	Revise data collection protocols as necessary.
	Compare and contrast results of quantitative data analysis and preliminary qualitative data.
	Write data and prepare preliminary interpretations.
	Draft interim report, incorporating both qualitative and quantitative data.
	Distribute interim report.
Months 7 & 8	Corroborate results across multiple groups and debrief interim report with participants.
	Collect additional interview data.
	Review new data and interim results.
	Write next draft of report.
	Seek feedback on report from ISES planning team.
	Prepare final report.
	Share results with appropriate campus community members.
Month 9	Design action plans and next steps.

In contrast, the typical timeline for producing a "final" site visit report during Project DEEP was about four months (Appendix B). Those interested in additional detailed information about DEEP site visit inquiries should review Appendix A of *Student Success in College*.

Although the ISES timeline outlined in Table 5.1 implies a linear process, with a beginning and end, the ethos of continuous improvement characteristic of DEEP schools is woven into the professional lives of institutional members and embedded into the campus culture. As a consequence, one of the positive side effects of implementing ISES is cultivating an orientation to continual self-reflection. After implementing two or three ISES cycles, say four or five years apart, such self-assessment might become a part of the institutional culture.

Human and Financial Resources

The kind and amounts of resources needed for ISES depend on the scope of the inquiry and whether one or more outside consultants will be involved. Creating a steering committee composed of well-regarded faculty, staff, and students is a good idea. This group might manage most of the project and prepare reports, but involving others in the data collection and vetting of results is essential. The steering committee should be led by someone who is widely respected and knowledgeable about the institution; reporting to a senior-level administrative officer can help ensure project accountability and credibility. Also, whatever the organizing group, staff support is necessary to obtain materials, help schedule interviews and focus groups, and arrange meetings and other events related to the project. Costs for meeting spaces and other venues should be budgeted along with modest support for refreshments for focus groups and debriefing meetings (see Appendix A, *Student Success in College*)—especially those that involve students!

If insiders alone are implementing ISES, additional compensation or release time might not be required, as is the case for a strategic planning process or an accreditation self-study. But if the scope is ambitious and the project spans two or more academic terms, other accommodations, such as additional resources and extra compensation, might be necessary to accomplish the work within the proposed timeline.

As discussed in Principle Six in Chapter Two, outside consultants might provide expertise not available within the institution. "Outsiders" also might be needed to help explore areas or issues that are too sensitive for insiders to probe effectively or to provide expertise, status, and credibility. Whatever the reasons, using outsiders requires additional financial resources. This can be money well spent if it produces a credible, balanced, and thorough review.

With or without external consultants, the group charged to coordinate and implement ISES must agree among themselves and with other key stakeholders about the desired outcomes of the project. In addition to written reports for institutional audiences, other "products" might be generated, including presentations to groups of faculty and students, governing boards, accreditors, philanthropic organizations, and community leaders.

This abbreviated overview of logistical considerations indicates that ISES requires a substantial commitment of human and financial resources. Among the most important of these are the will and resolve of key institutional leaders to improve undergraduates' experiences.

Applications of ISES

The ISES approach described up to this point represents a comprehensive, institutionwide examination of factors and conditions that influence student engagement and desirable outcomes of college. The rationale and principles on which ISES is based can be tailored to address challenges facing one or more institutional units or functions.

This section describes a handful of possible uses to illustrate how the concepts and steps embodied in the Inventory can be extended and tailored to selected areas of college and university life, including:

Academic administrators

Curriculum committees

Student Affairs professionals

Faculty and staff development

Admissions and student recruitment

Assessment and institutional research

Accreditation and self-studies

Campus partnerships

Strategic planning

Campus planning and development

Governing boards

Academic Administrators

Academic administrators oversee the curriculum and other learning experiences of students. At some institutions, undergraduate education is the primary mission; in other settings multiple missions are legitimate and must be carefully balanced. Assuming that you wish to cultivate an "unshakeable focus on student learning" as described in Section II (Chapter Three) and Chapter Three of *Student Success in College*), to what extent is this commitment manifested? And in what areas are improvements needed? Other chapters in the *Student Success* book worth reviewing include Two, Seven, Eight, and Ten along with their counterpart sections in this volume.

The following are aspects of institutional functioning that academic administrators might explore with faculty when designing planning exercises, retreats, or other activities dedicated to identifying ways to enrich student learning.

- *Mission:* What is the role of undergraduate education at our institution? Who reminds people of the importance of undergraduate education? Whose voices serve as the conscience of the campus when it comes to students and their success?

- *Vision:* What is the vision of faculty and staff for the student experience at our school? Has this vision changed over time? If so, how and why? Are mechanisms in place to review the vision on a periodic basis as the institution evolves?

- *Performance expectations:* Are the performance expectations for everyone on campus set at high but achievable levels? How are these standards measured for students? For faculty members? For administrators? For staff members?

- *Academic challenge:* Is academic rigor appropriate to students' academic preparation and the institution's learning goals?

- *Pedagogy:* Are faculty and others knowledgeable about the academic backgrounds of students? Do instructional approaches complement students' learning styles? Is support available to help faculty assess students' learning styles and develop appropriate pedagogical approaches?

Curriculum Committees

Groups charged with studying and revising existing curricular offerings and pedagogical practices on campus often encounter resistance to their recommendations. Some of this resistance can be countered with information about, for example, student course-taking patterns, learning outcomes, and student engagement data. Topics relevant to this issue are discussed in Section II (Chapter Three) and Chapter Three of *Student Success in College*. Other chapters in the *Student Success* book worth reviewing include Two, Seven, Eight, and Ten along with their counterpart sections in this volume.

Here are several issues that a curriculum review committee might consider to increase the odds of bringing about productive changes that enhance student learning and success:

- *Alignment of curricular content and mission:* Are the organization and content of the curriculum consistent with the institution's mission and goals for undergraduate education? What do current students and graduates say about the quality of their courses and other educational experiences?

- *Financial incentives and support for continuous improvement:* Are faculty members expected to revise, and are they rewarded for revising, courses on an annual basis? Are they expected to experiment, and are they rewarded for experimenting, with promising pedagogical approaches? What funding sources are available to support new initiatives?

- *Exposure to diverse perspectives:* Are diverse ways of thinking and knowing infused throughout the curriculum? Who champions the inclusion of diverse perspectives in the curriculum?

- *Decisions informed by data:* What information is available to point to needed changes to the curriculum and pedagogical approaches? Are students placed in appropriate courses based on their academic backgrounds? What do data indicate about existing general education and major field course requirements? How is student learning measured in general education and major fields?

Student Affairs Professionals

Student affairs professionals and others who provide student academic and social support services are key partners in supporting student success. According to *Powerful Partnerships* (American Association for Higher Education, American College Personnel Association, & National Association for Student Personnel Administrators, 1998), "only when everyone on campus—particularly academic affairs and student affairs—shares the responsibility for student learning will we be able to make significant progress in improving it" (p. 1). To identify features important to student success, pay special attention to campus life questions in ISES Section I, III, and in particular, all the questions related to psychological environments, and questions in Section IV and Section VI. Used in concert with Chapters Two, Four, Five, and Seven of *Student Success in College,* these questions prompt student affairs leaders to look at how their units can and should contribute to student learning and the life of the campus. They also can be used to organize a staff retreat or series of discussions about the functions and services of academic and student support units, including tutoring centers, writing labs, math labs, academic and career advisors, and centers for students from groups historically underrepresented in higher education.

Consider, for example, a student retention committee with the broad charge of creating better approaches to academic and social support for students. To determine whether enough effective safety nets exist for different groups of students (Chapters Seven and Twelve of *Student Success in College*), the committee might consider the following issues:

- *Committee composition:* Are people from different units who have different perspectives on the student experience represented? Are academic and student affairs staff members equally invested in the task? Are students, librarians, tutors, and instructional technology staff members involved with the effort? Who else should be involved or have input into the task?

- *Guiding assumptions:* What is your institution's operating philosophy regarding students' preparation, talents, and academic potential? Do people in different units share this view? Is the dominant view consistent with students' academic and social needs and the institution's mission?

- *Student perceptions:* Do students believe the institution is committed to their success? What messages do faculty, staff, and administrators send to students about what they need to do to perform at acceptable levels? Are different messages sent to different groups of students?

- *Interventions:* What practices and programs reach out to at-risk students? What do students know about these programs and what value do students place on the initiatives?

Faculty and Staff Development

As we discussed in *Student Success in College,* faculty development specialists have much to contribute to creating learning environments that support student success. Institutional workshops and other professional development experiences they organize can be indispensable to helping new and senior full-time and part-time faculty, teaching assistants, and staff hone pedagogical skills. Also, because faculty development specialists often do not represent the interests of individual departments or units, they can play a neutral role in facilitating potentially divisive conversations about the strengths and weaknesses of the institution's learning environment (Kuh, Schuh, Whitt, & Associates, 1991; Pascarella & Terenzini, 2005). Section II of ISES provides a series of questions related to improving student learning. Also suitable for organizing faculty and staff development activities are topics addressed in Clear Pathways to Student Success (Section IV, Chapter Three) and the Active and Collaborative Learning and Student-Faculty Interaction sections (Chapter Four) of ISES, and Chapters Three, Five, Nine, Ten, and Eleven of *Student Success in College.* These ideas also can be adapted for use at the college, school, department, or unit level to frame discussions about pedagogy and strategies to improve student learning.

Among the topics that warrant attention:

- *Areas of strength and concern:* What aspects of teaching and learning do assessments of student engagement suggest need attention, such as active and collaborative learning or enriching educational experiences? Which of these areas should be priorities for faculty development efforts? What is the campus doing well?

- *Alignment of teaching approaches and student learning styles:* What pedagogical strategies are more and less effective with students from different backgrounds and with different learning styles?

- *Collaboration:* What are targets of opportunity for increasing collaboration across functional areas to enhance student learning, such as between academic and student affairs?

Admissions and Student Recruitment

A good fit between student expectations and campus environments is associated with student satisfaction and engagement. For this reason, a college or university must describe the nature of students' experiences accurately and provide information about what students must do to survive and thrive during and following the first college year. Admissions materials, campus visits, Web sites, and other recruitment tools should be reviewed in the context of these questions to make sure the institution communicates accurate expectations and experiences to new students. Orientation processes should build on the information provided to students by the admissions office about what to expect from college and what it takes to achieve academic and social success at the institution. ISES Section IV (Chapter Three) and Chapter Five in *Student Success in College* raise important issues about transition programs to help new students make a successful shift from their previous college environment and enhance their success. Questions in the Acculturation section (Chapter Three) are especially important in this regard.

As you look ahead to the next student recruitment season, what messages does your institution send—intentionally or unintentionally—about:

- *Student success behaviors:* What is the image of the successful student projected by your printed admissions materials, the institutional Web site, and by campus tour guides? To what extent does the projected image accurately portray academic expectations and influence students' decisions to enroll, persist, and graduate?

- *Acculturation and acclimation:* How do prospective students learn about what it takes for academic success? Are they able to find one or more affinity groups that provide social support? What do transition events and materials communicate to different groups of students about institutional values, academic expectations, and the extent to which they are welcome and affirmed? How do these experiences introduce students to campus resources and opportunities?

- *Student engagement and persistence:* How much do admissions personnel know and share with prospective students about student engagement as measured by NSSE or other instruments? To what extent do admissions personnel discuss persistence and graduation rate information with prospective students?

Assessment and Institutional Research

The growing interest in student success makes the work of assessment officers and institutional researchers more important than ever. Relevant, usable data must be collected, interpreted, and reported so they are accessible and point to possible interventions. One immediate implication of research on fostering student success is the need for information about how groups on campus use assessment results and institutional research, including a focus on whether the appropriate people receive and review these reports and how they are used for improvement. Pertinent questions for such a task are raised in ISES Section V (Improvement-Oriented Ethos) supported by information from Chapter Six of *Student Success in College* to identify what data are collected, for what purposes, how they are used, and by whom. A more comprehensive approach takes the form of a campus culture audit based on the ISES Ultimately, It's About the Culture section (Chapter Three) and Chapters Two, Thirteen, and Fourteen of *Student Success in College*. A more focused inquiry could examine academic rigor guided by the ISES Academic Challenge section (Chapter Two) and Chapter Eight of *Student Success in College*.

A particularly important and instructive approach for identifying areas where improvement might be needed is to estimate the extent to which opportunities for student engagement exist across the institution, comparing and contrasting the experiences of different groups of students using the Enriching Educational Experiences section (Chapter Four) of ISES and Chapter Eleven of *Student Success in College*. The project could focus on:

- *Retention and graduation rates:* Do members of different groups have different graduation and retention rates? If so, what contributes to these differences?

- *Engagement:* Does engagement differ by race or ethnicity and/ or gender? Are there differences between students historically underserved by higher education and majority students in levels of engagement, academic challenge, or perceptions of a supportive campus environment? How do levels of engagement relate to persistence and graduation rates? Do different groups participate at the same levels in educationally enriching activities, such as internships, study abroad, service learning, and peer tutoring? How can those who do not participate be encouraged to do so? Do members of different groups seem to benefit differently from the experiences?

- *Campus environments:* Do members of different student groups experience or perceive the campus the same way? Are some groups more satisfied with the amount of academic and social support than are other groups? Are some less satisfied? What accounts for these differences?

In addition to ISES and *Student Success in College,* many other excellent resources offer helpful suggestions for how assessment officers and institutional researchers can document students' experiences and institutional factors associated with student success in college. They include Astin (1991); Banta, Lund, Black, and Oblander (1996); Kuh, Schuh, Whitt, and Associates (1991); and Upcraft and Schuh (1996).

Accreditation and Self-Studies

Regional and discipline-specific accreditors welcome institutional self-studies that are mission-sensitive and focus on student learning outcomes. Although accreditation processes typically focus on past and present institutional performance, several groups have emphasized the forward-looking aspects of accreditation. That is, what does the institution plan to do to improve specified areas of performance? For example, the Commission on Colleges Southern Association of Colleges and Schools (SACS) Quality Enhancement Plan (QEP) complements the institution's ongoing assessment and planning processes by encouraging schools to develop a focused plan that responds to local concerns about student learning along with a course of action to address them and enhance its educational effectiveness. ISES could be used to identify critical issues for student success and as a framework for documenting quality in the educational program. Bringing people together from different units to participate in the process can help build consensus about efforts to enhance quality. In addition, institutions may find the six properties and conditions outlined in *Student Success in College* useful as an organizing framework for accreditation self-study, as has Alverno College.

ISES and *Student Success in College* are well suited for guiding the development of the self-study. Particularly useful are ISES Sections I, II, and V (Chapter Three). Also instructive are Chapters Two, Three, and Six from *Student Success in College.* Areas on which to focus include:

- *Overlaps between espoused and enacted mission:* To what extent does what the institution communicates about itself comport with what students experience? To what degree are the practices, programs, and policies of specific divisions aligned with the mission of the unit and institution?

- *Institutional resources:* Are sufficient resources allocated to support the institution's commitment to student success? Do reallocation patterns reflect institutional values and priorities? If not, why?

- *Evidence of learning outcomes:* Are curricular outcomes consistent with goals? What measures are used to document this? Which units are able to demonstrate their contributions to student learning outcomes?

- *Enhancing the quality of programs and services:* How have data informed institutional improvement initiatives? To what extent are assessment activities integrated into programs and services? How is information about the quality of students' experience used to draw conclusions about the efficacy of campus initiatives?

Campus Partnerships

Shared responsibility for student success is a feature common to DEEP schools (Kinzie & Kuh, 2004; Kuh et al., 2005). One of the reasons for this is the number of strong on- and off-campus partnerships they have developed. These collaborative efforts extend beyond academic and student affairs and beyond the physical boundaries of the campus. For example, undergraduate students, librarians, IT staff, food service workers, building and grounds personnel, and others work in concert to achieve the educational mission of their institutions and conserve financial resources in the process. In addition, DEEP institutions forge partnerships with their community by linking people and resources to address issues that affect the quality of life on and off the campus and by offering many opportunities to enhance student learning, consistent with the advice of many observers who have examined this issue (AAHE, ACPA, & NASPA, 1998; Bacon, 2002; Daniel & Scott, 2001; Dietz & Enchelmayer, 2001; Fear & Doberneck, 2004; McDonald, 2002; Roper & Longerbeam, 2002; Schroeder, 1999a, 1999b; Schuh & Whitt, 1999; Seymour, 1995; Snyder, 2002).

ISES Section VI (Chapter Three) along with the Enriching Educational Experiences section (Chapter Four) combined with Chapters Seven and Eleven of *Student Success in College* can be used to guide discussions about the current state of productive partnerships on- and off-campus and how to identify elements that facilitate or impede partnerships for learning.

Some instructive areas to pursue are:

- *Partnerships that ensure effective student transitions:* To what extent are faculty members, academic administrators, first-year program personnel, new student orientation staff, student organization members, and parent groups working together effectively to develop transition experiences for new students?

- *Partnerships that enhance student learning:* To what extent do faculty members, career center staff, and community service agencies collaborate to facilitate high-quality learning experiences for students? What barriers exist to this collaboration? What factors facilitate collaboration?

- *Partnerships that promote leadership development:* To what extent do academic departments such as management, political science, and sociology work with staff in first-year programs, women's affairs, multicultural opportunity offices, residence life, or student organizations and activities to promote leadership development of students?

- *Partnerships that connect learning and work:* To what extent are financial aid, career planning and placement, external relations, student academic services, and local businesses working together to provide opportunities for educationally meaningful work experiences for students? How might they be improved?

Strategic Planning

When done well, strategic planning entails a thoughtful, comprehensive review of what an institution has done and what it proposes to do over the period of time the plan covers. Because ISES provides for a careful analysis of what the institution means to current members and stakeholders of the campus community, it is well suited to discussions in preparation for planning. Salient sections of ISES for this purpose are I and II (Chapter Three) together with Chapters Two and Three of *Student Success in College.* The material covered in these sections focuses on the institution's mission and core values, what an institution has done and what it proposes to do in the future to implement its mission, and stakeholders' long-term visions for the institution. For example:

- *Espoused and enacted missions:* Is what the institution espouses consistent with what actually occurs? If not, what can be done to align them? How can the mission be used to position the institution favorably for the next five to ten years?

- *Vision:* What does the institution aspire to be? How does the vision influence decision and policymaking? For how long will the vision remain appropriate, given predicted changes in the external environment?

- *Values:* How are institutional values used to inform campus planning and decision making? Have they been applied consistently over time? How are institutional values demonstrated in daily activities of institutional leaders, faculty and members, and students?

- *Pockets of excellence:* What programs are of especially high quality in fostering student success and must be preserved?

- *Targets of opportunity:* What programs and practice must be added or improved to ensure that more students will have access to the resources they need to succeed? What is the best way to identify and fund these activities?

Campus Planning and Development

Any place can be a "good place" for a college. Both the physical and psychological features of the campus environment affect how students feel about the institution and the effort they put into their studies. For example, where classrooms and faculty offices are placed and how they are designed can promote or discourage student-faculty interaction. Facilities can be created in ways that are user friendly and feel psychologically manageable, or that hinder access or comfort. For these reasons, campus planners should keep student learning and success at the forefront of their thinking when planning new buildings and renovating existing structures. Section III (Chapter Three) of ISES and Chapter Four of *Student Success in College* pose questions relevant to creating and maintaining physical and psychological environments oriented to fostering student success.

Included among the relevant areas to consider when taking stock of the location and physical and psychological properties of your institution and how they influence students' experiences are:

- *Location:* How does the institution use its setting to educational advantage? Are there aspects of the physical environment that make the campus feel "special" to students? How are these used to the institution's advantage?

- *Town-gown connections:* What does the institution do to identify and connect students with learning opportunities in the local community and surrounding area? Has it cultivated a core of institutional friends and advocates off campus with whom joint initiatives could be developed to involve more students and enrich their learning?

- *Psychological size:* When new buildings are planned or facilities renovated, what is done to ensure that they feel welcoming and are not overwhelming? To what extent do newcomers, students, and others report that the institution is difficult to navigate? How do they learn to deal with the complexities of the campus? What can be done to make the institution more easily understood?

- *Psychological climate:* Do some groups of students feel more "at home" at the institution than others? What accounts for these differing feelings of acceptance and comfort with the setting? Do people who are not members of the majority culture feel welcomed? How are their differences celebrated? Do they feel they are full partners and members in the institution?

Governing Boards

Governing board members are responsible for ensuring the vitality of the institution, consistent with its educational mission and aspirations. Yet, few board members have first-hand experience with college or university governance structures and processes. The issues raised in Section I (Chapter Three) of the ISES and Chapters One and Two of *Student Success in College* could help them learn about and understand aspects of the institution necessary for them to govern effectively. Board members seeking ways to evaluate their institution's performance can use the questions in ISES Section VI (Chapter Three) and Chapters Seven and Thirteen of *Student Success in College*. These ideas also could provide the basis for a productive board retreat or extended conversation about student success at their institution. Other topics that warrant board attention are:

- *Mission and values:* Are the espoused and enacted missions of the institution consistent? If not, in what ways are they inconsistent, and what impact do the inconsistencies have on student success? What are the institution's core values about students and their education? How do you know if you are achieving the mission?

- *Leadership priorities:* Where among the president's priorities do students, their learning, and their success fall? What does the president say and do in the name of promoting student success and the conditions that are associated with student success? What do institutional leaders do to model and symbolize the importance of students and the educational mission of the institution?

- *Faculty and staff priorities:* To what extent do faculty and staff devote their time and energies to activities that address the student success aspects of the mission?

- *Board priorities:* Where do students and their learning fall among the governing board's priorities? To what extent do students feel they and their success are institutional priorities? What roles do students play in campus governance, institutional planning, and faculty and staff recruitment and selection? What mechanisms or structures does the board use to promote and support student participation in decision making or program development? Does the culture of the board encourage or discourage open, productive dialogue about these and other matters related to student success (Kuh, 2005)?

A Last Word

ISES is a work in progress. We developed it to stimulate reflection, conversation, and action based on findings from the DEEP project and other studies of high-performing colleges and universities, student engagement, and institutional improvement. Although any institution can benefit from the probing, self-regarding queries in ISES, the process yields the most useful results in settings where students and their learning are among the institution's highest priorities and where enough people are ready to evaluate the status quo. Campus constituents must be willing to invest time and energy. They need to reculture the institution to cultivate an ethos of continuous improvement with student success as the goal (Fullan, 2001).

Having learned a great deal from Project DEEP campuses, we trust that other institutions can benefit from the policies and practices described in *Student Success in College* and in this volume. At the same time, as increasingly diverse waves of new students pursue postsecondary education, we must redouble our efforts to discover what matters to student learning and success. Working together we can increase what we know about effective educational practice and ways to improve student and institutional performance.

Toward these ends, we invite you to share with us how you are using ISES and how it might be improved. We look forward to hearing from and working with you.

REFERENCES

Adelman, C. (2004). *Principal indicators of student academic histories in postsecondary education, 1972–2000.* Washington, DC: U.S. Department of Education, Institute of Education Sciences.

American Association for Higher Education (AAHE), American College Personnel Association (ACPA), & National Association of Student Personnel Administrators (NASPA). (1998). *Powerful partnerships: A shared responsibility for learning.* Washington, DC: American College Personnel Association.

Astin, A. W. (1984). Student involvement: A developmental theory for higher education. *Journal of College Student Personnel, 25,* 297–308.

Astin, A. W. (1985). *Achieving educational excellence.* San Francisco: Jossey-Bass.

Astin, A. W. (1991). Assessment *for excellence: The philosophy and practice of assessment and evaluation in higher education.* American Council on Education Series on Higher Education. Washington, DC/New York: American Council on Education and Macmillan.

Astin, A. W. (1993). *What matters in college? Four critical years revisited.* San Francisco: Jossey-Bass.

Bacon, J. L. (2002). Promoting community through citizenship and service. In W. M. McDonald & Associates, *Creating campus community: In search of Ernest Boyer's legacy* (pp. 121–144). San Francisco: Jossey-Bass.

Banta, T. W., Lund, J. P., Black, K. E., & Oblander, F. W. (1996). *Assessment in practice: Putting principles to work on college campuses.* San Francisco: Jossey-Bass.

Bolman, L. G., & Deal, T. E. (2003). *Reframing organizations: Artistry, choice, and leadership.* (3rd ed.) San Francisco: Jossey-Bass.

Bruffee, K. A. (1993). *Collaborative learning: Higher education, interdependence, and the authority of knowledge.* Baltimore: The Johns Hopkins University Press.

Carey, K. (2004). *A matter of degrees: Improving graduation rates in four year colleges and universities.* Washington, DC: Education Trust.

Chaffee, E., & Tierney, W. G. (1988). *Collegiate culture and leadership strategy.* New York: Macmillan.

Chickering, A. W., & Gamson, Z. F. (1987). Seven principles for good practice in undergraduate education. *AAHE Bulletin, 39*(7), 3–7.

Chickering, A. W., & Reisser, L. (1993). *Education and identity.* San Francisco: Jossey-Bass.

Collins, J. C. (2001). *Good to great.* New York: Harper-Collins.

Cooperrider, D. L., & Srivastva, S. (1987). Appreciative inquiry in organizational life. *Research in Organizational Change and Development, I,* 129–169.

Daniel, B. V., & Scott, B. R. (2001). (Eds.). *Consumers, adversaries, and partners: Working with the families of undergraduates.* New Directions for Student Services, no. 94. San Francisco: Jossey-Bass.

Dietz, L. H., & Enchelmayer, E. T. (Eds.). (2001). *Developing external partnerships for cost-effective enhanced service.* New Directions for Student Services, no. 90. San Francisco: Jossey-Bass.

Ely, M., & Associates. (1991). *Doing qualitative research: Circles within circles.* New York: Falmer.

Fear, F. A., & Doberneck, D. M. (2004). Collegial talk: A powerful tool for change. *About Campus, 9*(1), 11–19.

Fullan, M. (2001). *Leading in a culture of change.* San Francisco: Jossey-Bass.

Goodsell, A. M., Maher, M., & Tinto, V. (Eds.). (1992). *Collaborative learning: A sourcebook for higher education.* University Park, PA: National Center on Postsecondary Teaching, Learning, and Assessment, The Pennsylvania State University.

Johnson, D. W., Johnson, R., & Smith, K. A. (1991). *Cooperative learning: Increasing college faculty instructional productivity.* ASHE-ERIC Higher Education Report No. 4. Washington, DC: The George Washington University, School of Education and Human Development.

Kinzie, J., & Kuh, G. D. (2004). Going DEEP: Learning from campuses that share responsibility for student success. *About Campus, 9*(5), 2–8.

Kuh, G. D. (1990). Assessing student culture. In W. G. Tierney (Ed.), *Assessing academic climates and cultures.* New Directions for Institutional Research, no. 68. San Francisco: Jossey-Bass.

Kuh, G. D. (1993). Appraising the character of a college. *Journal of Counseling and Development, 71*, 661–668.

Kuh, G. D. (2004). Forging a new direction: How UTEP created its own brand of excellence. *About Campus, 9*(5), 9–15.

Kuh, G. D. (2005). 7 steps for taking student learning seriously. *Trusteeship, 13*(3), 20–24.

Kuh, G. D., & Andreas, R. E. (1991). It's about time: Using qualitative research methods in student affairs. *Journal of College Student Development, 32*, 397–405.

Kuh, G. D., Kinzie, J., Schuh, J. H., Whitt, E. J., & Associates. (2005). *Student success in college: Creating conditions that matter.* San Francisco: Jossey-Bass.

Kuh, G. D., Schuh, J. H., & Whitt, E. J. (1991). Some good news about campus life: How "Involving Colleges" promote learning outside the classroom. *Change, 23*(5), 48–55.

Kuh, G. D., Schuh, J. H., Whitt, E. J., & Associates. (1991). *Involving colleges: Successful approaches to fostering student learning and personal development outside the classroom.* San Francisco: Jossey-Bass.

Kuh, G. D., & Whitt, E. J. (1988). *The invisible tapestry: Culture in American colleges and universities.* ASHE-ERIC Higher Education Report, No. 1. Washington, DC: Association for the Study of Higher Education.

Lawrence-Lightfoot, S. (1997). Illumination: Framing the terrain. In S. Lawrence-Lightfoot & J. Hoffman Davis, *The art and science of portraiture* (pp. 41–59). San Francisco: Jossey-Bass.

Magolda, P. M. (1999). Using ethnographic fieldwork and case studies to guide student affairs practice. *Journal of College Student Development, 40*(1), 10–21.

Martin, J. (2002). *Organizational culture: Mapping the terrain.* Thousand Oaks, CA: Sage.

McDonald, W. M. (2002). Absent voices: Assessing students' perceptions of campus community. In W. M. McDonald & Associates, *Creating campus community: In search of Ernest Boyer's legacy* (pp. 145–168). San Francisco: Jossey-Bass.

McKeachie, W. J., Pintrich, P. R., Lin, Y., & Smith, D. (1986). *Teaching and learning in the college classroom: A review of the research.* Ann Arbor: National Center for Research to Improve Postsecondary Teaching and Learning, University of Michigan.

Merriam, S. B., & Associates (2002). *Qualitative research in practice: Examples for discussion and analysis.* San Francisco: Jossey-Bass.

Pascarella, E. T. (2001). Identifying excellence in undergraduate education: Are we even close? *Change, 33*(3), 19–23.

Pascarella, E. T., & Terenzini, P. T. (1991). *How college affects students.* San Francisco: Jossey-Bass.

Pascarella, E. T., & Terenzini, P. T. (2005). *How college affects students: A third decade of research, Volume 2.* San Francisco: Jossey-Bass.

Patton, M. Q. (2002). *Qualitative research and evaluation methods.* (3rd ed.) Thousand Oaks, CA: Sage.

Pike, G. R. (1993). The relationship between perceived learning and satisfaction with college: An alternative view. *Research in Higher Education, 34*(1), 23–40.

Roper, L. D., & Longerbeam, S. D. (2002). Modeling community through campus leadership. In W. M. McDonald & Associates, *Creating campus community: In search of Ernest Boyer's legacy* (pp. 69–92). San Francisco: Jossey-Bass.

Rosovsky, H. (1990). *The university: An owner's manual.* New York: W. W. Norton.

Rossman, G. B., & Rallis, S. F. (2003). *Learning in the field: An introduction to qualitative research.* (2nd ed.) Thousand Oaks, CA: Sage.

Schroeder, C. C. (1999a). Partnerships: An imperative for enhancing student learning and institutional effectiveness. In J. H. Schuh & E. J. Whitt (Eds.), *Creating successful partnerships between academic and student affairs.* New Directions for Student Services, no. 87 (pp. 5–18). San Francisco: Jossey-Bass.

Schroeder, C. C. (1999b). Forging educational partnerships that advance student learning. In G. S. Blimling, E. J. Whitt, & Associates, *Good practice in student affairs: Principles to foster student learning* (pp. 133–156). San Francisco: Jossey-Bass.

Schuh, J. H., & Kuh, G. D. (1991, Winter). Evaluating the quality of collegiate environments. *Journal of College Admission, 130,* 17–22.

Schuh, J. H., & Upcraft, M. L. (2000). *Assessment practice in student affairs: An applications manual.* San Francisco: Jossey-Bass.

Schuh, J. H., & Whitt, E. J. (Eds.). (1999). *Creating successful partnerships between academic and student affairs.* New Directions for Student Services, no. 87. San Francisco: Jossey-Bass.

Seymour, D. (1995). *Once upon a campus: Lessons for improving quality and productivity in higher education.* American Council on Higher Education Series on Higher Education. Phoenix, AZ: Oryx.

Snyder, M. B. (Ed.) (2002). *Student affairs and external relations.* New Directions for Student Services, no. 100. San Francisco: Jossey-Bass.

Sorcinelli, M. D. (1991). Research findings on the Seven Principles. In A. W. Chickering & Z. F. Gamson (Eds.), *Applying the Seven Principles for Good Practice in undergraduate education.* New Directions for Teaching and Learning (pp. 13–25). San Francisco: Jossey-Bass.

Terenzini, P. T., & Pascarella, E. T. (1994). Living with myths: Undergraduate education in America. *Change, 26*(1), 28–32.

Tierney, W. G. (1999). *Building the responsive campus: Creating high performance colleges and universities.* Thousand Oaks, CA: Sage.

Upcraft, M. L., & Schuh, J. H. (1996). *Assessment in student affairs: A guide for practitioners.* San Francisco: Jossey-Bass.

Weick, K. E. (1984). Small wins. *American Psychologist, 39*(1), 40–49.

Weick, K. E. (1995). *Sensemaking in organizations.* Thousand Oaks, CA: Sage.

Whitt, E. J. (1993). "Making the familiar strange": Discovering culture. In G. D. Kuh (Ed.), *Using cultural perspectives in student affairs work* (pp. 81–94). Washington, D.C.: American College Personnel Association.

Whitt, E. J. (1996). Assessing student cultures. In M. L. Upcraft, J. H. Schuh, & Associates, *Assessment in student affairs* (pp. 189–216). San Francisco: Jossey-Bass.

Whitt, E. J., & Kuh, G. D. (1991). Qualitative research in higher education: A team approach to multiple site investigation. *Review of Higher Education, 14,* 317–337.

ISES: Suggested Interview Protocols

Questions/Approaches for Students

- Tell us about yourself—your name, year, major, why you chose [institution], and why you have stayed.

- What did you expect at [institution] and why? In what ways were your expectations met? What didn't go as expected?

- What would you say to a prospective student about the strengths and weaknesses of being a student here?

- What are the highlights of your academic experience?

- What are the highlights of your entire experience? What would you change if you could?

- How would you describe the level of academic challenge here? In required courses outside your major? In your major field classes? What has been particularly challenging for you about being a student here?

- What campus activities have you been involved in? What have you learned from them? Is it easy or difficult to get involved?

- For student leaders: Do you recall who on campus first pulled you into campus activities? What have you gained from those experiences?

- What's important at this institution? What does it value?

- What have you learned from being a student here? How did that learning occur?

- To whom do you turn most often when you need academic help? Why?

- What does it mean to you to be a successful student at [institution]? Why do you define success here in that way?
- What resources and services are available to help you be successful? To what extent have you taken advantage of them?
- Talk about one class that impressed you. Does another class come to mind? Tell me about that one, too.
- If you were the admissions director here, what personal traits would you look for in candidates for admission? Why?
- Talk about your interactions with faculty. To what extent have you spent time with faculty out of class? How many faculty members could you ask to write a meaningful letter of recommendation for you and how have you created those relationships?
- How do you spend your weekends?
- How do you spend your time during the week? What would be a typical day for you?
- When you talk with your friends over breaks, or through e-mail, or on the phone, how does the rigor of your college experience compare with theirs?
- How much opportunity have you had to interact with students who have different backgrounds and experiences from you?
- Have you participated in any internships, field experiences, community service work, or study abroad? Tell me about one of these activities.
- If you were in charge for a day and could change everything about this institution, what is the one thing you would not change? What is one thing you would change if you could?
- What campus traditions would you want to see alive and well when you return ten years from now as an alumna/us?

Questions/Approaches for Faculty

- Why did you come to [institution]? Why have you stayed?
- What is special about [institution]?
- What is the mission of [institution]? How do you know?
- How does the mission influence student learning and students' experiences? How does the mission influence your work as a faculty member?
- What does [institution] do particularly well? What are its most important shortcomings?
- What's it like to be a[n] [tenured/untenured/adjunct] faculty member here? Is that what you expected? How is it different from or similar to your expectations?

- What's valued for faculty here? What does it take to achieve tenure? How do you know?
- How do you spend your time? What would be a typical day for you?
- Describe the types of interactions you have with students in and outside the classroom. How and by whom are those interactions initiated?
- How would you describe [institution] students?
- How would you describe and evaluate the overall quality of undergraduates' experiences here? What words would you use to describe the student culture—or cultures?
- What constitutes student success at [institution]? How is success defined? How do you know? What do students have to do to be successful? To what extent are students successful? Which students are most successful?
- What aspects of the institution contribute to student learning and what aspects hinder it? What are some examples of outstanding programs and practices?
- How has [institution] changed in the past five years? What brought about these changes?
- To what extent do faculty and staff share ideas for improvement? How does that sharing occur?
- What particular practices at [institution] are distinctive and work especially well for different groups of students?
- Where has the campus invested its resources over the past few years? What impact have those investments had for faculty? For students?
- How do campus leaders foster institutional improvement? At what level are these changes initiated?
- To what extent does [institution] have and use information about students to improve student learning?
- If you were in charge for a day and could change everything about this institution, what is the one thing you would not change? What is the one thing you would change if you could?

Questions/Approaches for Staff and Administrators

- Why did you come to [institution]? Why have you stayed?
- What is special about [institution]?
- What is the mission of [institution]? How do you know?
- How does the mission influence student learning and students' experiences? How does the mission influence your work?

- What does [institution] do particularly well? What are its most significant shortcomings?
- What's it like to be a staff member here? Is that what you expected? How is it different or similar?
- What's valued for staff here? How do you know?
- How do you spend your time? What would be a typical day for you?
- Describe the types of interactions you have with students. How are those interactions initiated?
- How would you describe [institution] students?
- How would you describe and evaluate the overall quality of the undergraduate experience here? What words would you use to describe the student culture—or cultures?
- What constitutes student success at [institution]? How is success defined? How do you know? What do students have to do to be successful? To what extent are students successful? Which students are most successful? What role do you play in their success?
- What aspects of the institution contribute to student learning and what aspects hinder it? What are some examples of outstanding programs and practices?
- How has [institution] changed in the past five years and what brought about these changes?
- To what extent do faculty and staff share ideas for improvement? How does that sharing occur?
- What particular practices at [institution] are distinctive and work especially well for different groups of students?
- Where has the campus invested its resources over the past few years? What impact have those investments had for faculty? For students? For staff?
- How do campus leaders foster institutional improvement? At what level are these changes initiated?
- To what extent does [institution] have and use information about students to improve student learning?
- If you were in charge for a day and could change anything about this institution, what would be the one thing you would not change? What is one thing you would change if you could?

General Interview Probes

The following generic probes might help you get at a deeper level of meaning and uncover a variety of perspectives. Consider using them throughout your interview.

- Please share an example of what you are talking about.
- In what ways do you think [person, activity, program, environment, and so on] contributes to [outcome—engagement, success, persistence, and so on]?
- Do you think everyone shares this perspective?
- With whom else might I need to talk about this?
- Who might have a different opinion?
- Are there any documents that I should review?
- What should I know that I've not already asked you?
- Is there anything you expected me to ask that I haven't touched on? If so, what?

DEEP Site Visit Report Timeline

About four months was the norm for producing the Final Site Visit Report for DEEP schools. This included contacting, and describing the project to, the participating institution; forming a site visit team; preparing for the first visit; conducting the first site visit; preparing and distributing the interim report; planning and conducting the second site visit; and preparing and delivering the final report.

Dates	Task
Month 1	Identify site visit team members.
	Develop data collection approach and tools (e.g., interviews, case study method, action research).
	Identify all potential data sources.
	Devise protocols for interviews and focus groups, document analysis, and observations.
	Determine approach to recording and storing data.
	Obtain data collection aids (e.g., tape recorders, tapes).
	Secure Human Subjects/Institutional Review Committee approval.
Month 2	Train team to refine purpose and scope of research.
	Contact institutions and secure permission to conduct study.
	Coordinate site visit dates with institutional contact.

Dates	Task
	Communicate understanding of and information about the purposes of the visit, expected outcomes, and visit schedules to appropriate individuals on campus.
	Create schedule for site visit.
	Arrange locations for meetings and interviews.
	Assemble site visit team.
Month 3	Work with site visit coordinator to invite study participants.
	Review documents in advance of visit; prepare for study.
	Remind participants of study.
	Travel to site.
	Collect data on site.
	Discuss data collection and initial results with site visit team.
	Write field notes and interpretations.
Month 4	Complete interim report.
	Conduct second site visit and conduct debriefings with participants
	Revise report based on second visit, review with team.
	Write final report.
	Seek feedback on final report from institution.
	Create final report.
	Determine next steps.

A

Academic administrators, and institutional functioning, 66
Academic-student affairs partnerships, 38
Accreditation self-study, 73
Active and collaborative learning, 48–50; effective practices in, 48; and peer tutoring, 50; and student accountability, 50
Adelman, C., 3
Admissions materials, review of, 70
Alverno College, academic advising at, 58–59
American Association for Higher Education, 68, 74
Appreciative inquiry, and student engagement, 9
Assessment officers, research approaches for, 71–72

B

Baccalaureate attainment rates, 3
Bacon, J. L., 74
Banta, T. W., 11, 13, 72
Black, K. E., 11, 13, 72
Bolman, L. G., 13
Bruffee, K. A., 4

C

California State University at Monterey Bay (CSUMB): active and collaborative learning approaches at, 50; culture of engagement at, 42
Campus partnerships, 15, 38, 74–75
Campus environment: assessment of, 71–72; centrality of student success in, 39; conditions for student support in, 57; culture audit of, 71; human-scale design of, 28; and institutional effectiveness, 39–42; physical and psychological aspects of, 10, 25–28; and student recruitment, 70; for student support, 11, 57–59

Carey, K., 3
Chaffee, E., 14
Chickering, A. W., 4
College Student Experiences Questionnaire (CSEQ), 11
Collins, J. C., 15
Community-campus partnerships, 15, 38, 74–75
Continuous feedback, pedagogical practice of, 48
Cooperrider, D. L., 9
Critical thinking and writing skills, 45, 47
Curriculum committees, 67

D

Daniel, B. V., 74
Deal, T. E., 13
Diagnostic queries, 12; on acculturation, 29–30; on active and collaborative learning, 48–50; adaptation of, 9; on college mission/philosophy, 20–21; on enriching experiences, 54–55; on innovation and improvement efforts, 33–34; on institutional/student cultures and environments, 26–27, 40–41; and response formats, 18; on student learning focus, 22–24; on student-faculty interactions, 51–52; on student success, 29–31, 45–46; on transition and support programs, 57–58
Dietz, L. H., 74
Diversity: DEEP schools' support of, 26; learning opportunities created by, 53
Doberneck, D. M., 13
Documenting Effective Educational Practice (DEEP) project: improvement-oriented ethos and, 15; institutions studied in, 5–6; methodology, 6; outsider perspectives in, 14; purposes of, 5; student perspectives in, 13–14; and sustainable transformations, 15–16; testing assumptions in, 13